GOLD CAMP CALLED

SUMMITVILLE

BY
RICHARD C. HUSTON

WESTERN REFLECTIONS PUBLISHING COMPANY®

©2012 Richard C. Huston
All rights reserved in whole or in part

ISBN 978-1-937851-01-9
Library of Congress Number 2011946238

Cover and text design: FluiDESIGNS, Steve Smith

First Edition
Printed in the United States of America

Western Reflections Publishing Company®
P.O. Box 1149
951 N. Highway 149
Lake City, CO 81235
www.westernreflectionspublishing.com

Dedication

This book is dedicated to those individuals who lived and worked at Summitville, a gold camp high in the San Juan Mountains, and to Philip M. Bethke, a well-known geologist who played a significant role in researching and describing the unusual geology of the Summitville area.

Philip Martin Bethke, known as Phil to his friends, was appreciated and honored for his generosity and integrity. He was born in Chicago on March 22, 1930 and spent his youth in Winnetka, Illinois. At the age of eighteen he entered Amherst College where he majored in geology and played tight end on the football team. After graduation from Amherst he moved to New York City where he started graduate studies in geology at Columbia University. He received his master's degree in 1954. He and Jean McKay, also from Chicago, were married in New York City on May 28, 1955. Phil accepted the position of assistant professor at the Missouri School of Mines for four years. He completed his dissertation for a doctor of philosophy degree in geology from Columbia University in 1957. The first two of his seven children, Craig and Bruce, were born in Rolla, Missouri.

Phil left the Missouri School of Mines in the summer of 1959 and joined the U.S. Geological Survey to participate in the study of geology of the Creede ore deposits in Colorado's San Juan Mountains — the beginning of Phil's thirty-eight year career with the Geological Survey.

After Phil's first summer with the Survey, he moved his family to Bethesda, Maryland, where children Alison, Scott, Lynn, Andrew, and Leslie joined the Bethke family. Phil worked at the Washington D.C. Department of the Interior offices and then at the Geological Survey's Reston, Virginia National Center. He became the leader of the team studying the geology of the Creede ore deposits in order to better understand the anatomy and physiology of ore deposits. Phil spent summers in Creede, gathering information for the study. In fact, the Creede study yielded so many theses that the project was called "Creede University." The study of Summitville mineralization done by Phil, Bob Rye, Roger Stoffregen, and others' study of Summitville mineralization was a significant contribution to the understanding of acid-sulfate ore deposits in general and was a primary source of information used to describe Summitville and Upper Alamosa River Basin geology in this book.

Phil served on many Geological Survey internal committees; was organizer and then Acting Chief of the Computer Center Division (1966-67); and Chief of the Experimental Geochemistry and Petrology Branch (1980-83). He authored more than eighty peer-reviewed publications. He received the Interior Department's Meritorious Service Award in 1989.

Phil retired in 1995 and then contributed thousands of hours as a Scientist Emeritus, which included assembling the report on the scientific drilling project in the Creede caldera. The report, *Ancient Lake Creede*, was co-edited by Phil and Richard L. Hay and published by the Geological Society of America in 2000. Phil also served the Society of Economic Geologists as president and as a member of six committees. He was given the Interior Department's Distinguished Service Award in 1999.

After retiring from the Survey, Phil and his wife built a home overlooking the Rio Grande near Creede where they spent their summers and parts of some winters too He was a consultant with the Willow Creek Reclamation Project, was a member of the Creede Historical Society, and enjoyed local activities such as high school basketball games, the Creede Repertory Theater, and the annual gem and mineral shows.

Phil passed away suddenly on November 14, 2011 in Bethesda, Maryland and was honored at a memorial service in Washington, D.C. on November 19, 2011. A celebration of Phil's life will be held in Creede during the summer of 2012.

TABLE OF CONTENTS

DEDICATION.. i

PREFACE... 1

PROLOGUE... 9
    Summitville and Upper Alamosa River Basin Geology
    Weather

CHAPTER 1 – DISCOVERY (1870-1874).............................. 25
    Pear Joshua Peterson
    J. Carey French
    Del Norte

CHAPTER 2 – BONANZA (1875-1887)................................. 37
    Mines and Mills
    Mining Companies
    Thomas M. Bowen
    Summitville Town Site
    A Stagecoach Holdup

CHAPTER 3 – SLOW TIMES (1888-1926)............................ 71
    Albert Eugene Reynolds
    Theodore N. Barnsdall
    Mining Companies

CHAPTER 4 – REBIRTH (1926-1950)..................................... 82
    Pickens' Cut
    Summitville Mines Corporation
    Mines, Mills and Operating Companies
    High-Grading
    Life in Summitville

CHAPTER 5 –
    LIMITED PRODUCTION AND EXPLORATION
        (1950-1984)..126
    Limited Production
    Exploration
    The Summitville Gold Boulder
CHAPTER 6 –
    GALACTIC RESOURCES, INC. (1984-1992)..........138
    Open-Pit Mining and Heap Leaching
    Galactic's Mining and Milling Operations
    History of Galactic's Summitville Operations
APPENDICES..155
    Summitville Metal Production (1870-1992)
    Property Map, Summitville Mines, July 21, 1971

FOOTNOTES..160

BIBLIOGRAPHY..173

INDEX

PREFACE

Summitville is located in a remote part of Colorado's San Juan Mountains. I grew up in Monte Vista not far from Summitville and I remember neighbors and friends telling about life and times at Summitville. Other books have been written describing specific periods of time at Summitville, but none record its history from the beginning in 1870 to the last mining venture in the 1980s and 1990s that resulted in a disaster and an Environmental Protection Agency Superfund Site. This book is my attempt is to save Summitville's history, including activities that led to the Superfund Site declaration.

The first recorded production of gold from Colorado's Summitville Mining District was in 1871 and the last in 1992. The district produced 552,439 troy ounces of gold, 752,700 troy ounces of silver, 1,018,297 pounds of copper and 115,147 pounds of lead over a period of 121 years. The last nine years of Summitville mining, from 1984 through 1992, produced 294,365 troy ounces of gold and 319,814 troy ounces of silver, about half the district's total gold and silver production.

Troy ounces are used to record the weights of precious metals and gemstones. There are 14.583 troy ounces in the avoirdupois pound, which is used for weight measurement instead of 16 ounces normally used.

It is possible that the first gold production at Summitville was by an expedition of Frenchmen from 1799 to 1801. If the story of Treasure Mountain is in fact true, the gold produced from Summitville and other sites in present-day Colorado was hidden on Treasure Mountain as the Indians attacked the Frenchmen, killing most and forcing the rest out of the area. Treasure Mountain lies about thirteen miles west of Summitville and three miles south of the Wolf Creek Pass summit. There is physical evidence that strongly suggests the story of the French expeditions is authentic.

Maynard Cornett Adams, in his books *Citadel Mountain, Volumes I and II,* details the story of the French expeditions and Treasure Mountain. He describes physical evidence to back up the story. Perry Eberhart, in his book *Treasure Tales of the Rockies,* also tells the story.

This book's author knew Louie Bockhaus, who owned and operated a sawmill southwest of Monte Vista in the 1940s and 1950s. Louie spent his spare time searching for the treasure. He claimed the treasure was buried at the center of a triangle defined by three markers. Louie claimed he found two of the three but, unfortunately, not the third.

Two of the earliest and successful recorded discoveries of gold in the San Juan Mountains were made in the summer of 1870 at Summitville and in Arrastra Gulch in San Juan County. These two discoveries were the beginning of extensive prospecting in the San Juan Mountains that resulted in the discovery of many more mineral deposits. The first miners into the San Juans west of the 107th meridian were trespassing on Ute Indian land that had been assigned to the Utes by the Treaty of 1868. The Brunot Treaty of 1873 redeemed the miners by paying the Utes twelve cents an acre for their four million acres of San Juan mineral land. Summitville was not involved, since it lies east of the 107th meridian.

The Summitville Mining District is located high in the San Juan Mountains in the southwest corner of Rio Grande County. The mines were at elevations between 11,300 and 12,300 feet. The town site was at an elevation ranging from 11,200 to 11,400 feet above sea level.

The district is remote and connected to local towns by crooked mountain roads. Summitville is most easily reached by automobile by taking U.S. Highway 160 toward Wolf Creek Pass for eight miles past its intersection with State Highway 149 and then southerly about fourteen miles on U.S. Forest Service Road 380, a winding dirt road along Park Creek, to its junction with the Summitville Road. Take this road about three miles to Summitville. To go to the upper Alamosa River Basin, return to U.S. Forest Service Road 380, turn left and follow it to the Elwood Pass Road and then down to the upper Alamosa River Basin, a distance of about seven miles.

The nearest town is Del Norte, some thirty miles northeast of Summitville. A rough mountain road following Los Piños Creek connects Del Norte and Summitville.

At one time the route from Monte Vista to Summitville followed the Gunbarrel Road about two miles past the Huston farm, then went southwest to the Alamosa River and up the Alamosa River to its confluence with Wightman Fork. From there the road branched off the Alamosa River road and headed up Wightman Fork to Summitville. This section of the road is now impassable.

I grew up in Monte Vista and have many memories of people who worked at Summitville and of the Alamosa River and Summitville areas. My father owned a farm ten miles south of Monte Vista on Gunbarrel Road in the Bowen farming district. The district was named after Thomas M. Bowen, a Colorado senator who made his fortune at Summitville. Our family picnicked on Cat Creek (Rio Los Gatos as named by the early Spanish) along the road to the Alamosa River area in the fall of each year. We picked choke cherries that Mom made into delicious jelly.

As a child, I knew "Grandma Pfeiffer," daughter-in-law of Captain Albert Pfeiffer who was an Indian fighter and life-long friend of Kit Carson. My parents took me on Sunday afternoon drives and visits with Grandma, a gracious lady of about eighty years at that time. She let me play Indians in a beaded jacket with a bullet hole in the back. The jacket belonged to a Comanche chief killed by Pfeiffer and is now in the Rio Grande County Museum in Del Norte. On one Sunday afternoon drive up the Alamosa River, Grandma Pfeiffer pointed to a strawberry shaped hill and said that was where the troops sent heliograph signals from its top to Fort Garland when they were on patrol on the west side of the San Luis Valley. Many years later I confirmed that my remembrance was, indeed, a fact. The hill, Chiquita Peak, was a signal location.

The Huston family camped out along the Alamosa River in the late 1930s so Dad could cut down aspen trees with an axe to serve as rafters for the potato cellar he was building on the farm. Mom kept camp, a tent, and cooked meals over an open fire for Dad, my brother Joe, and me. I helped Dad trim bark off the poles with a drawknife. I drove past the farm several years ago and noticed that the potato cellar's roof had fallen in and the aspen poles we had so laboriously cut and skinned were standing out of the ruins of the cellar like ribs of a skeleton.

I remember taking trips up the Alamosa River past the Terrace Reservoir in the late 1930s. My father had a water right in the Terrace for his farm and he liked to see how much water was in the reservoir. I asked Dad why we never went fishing in the reservoir and he said there were no fish in it or in the Alamosa River. It was common knowledge in Monte Vista that there were no fish in the Alamosa below Horsethief Park.

My uncle, Homer Tyrrel, managed road construction projects for Rio Grande County and the U. S. Forest Service. He supervised upgrading the main road that followed the Alamosa River to Stunner and then the construction of the Stunner Pass road from the ghost town of Stunner over the mountain to Platoro on the Conejos River. An older cousin of mine, Homer Erickson, who spent the summer of 1934 with Homer and his wife Ida May, described his visit in a letter to me several years ago:

The summer of 1934 was a memorable one for me as I was privileged to spend it with Ida May and Homer Tyrrel. For a city boy this was an education on living in a bygone era. Homer was employed by the United States Forest Service to supervise road construction. He selected an abandoned miner's cabin as the place for the three of us to live which still had a wood stove for heat and cooking, a bed with springs, a table and chairs, and an old working gramophone with a record of "Alexander's Ragtime Band." A Coleman lantern supplied the light, the water supply from a spring 300 yards away, refrigeration from a wood frame draped with cotton fabric placed in a quiet part of the stream, and, last but not least, the plumbing, a two holer 30 yards away. The cabin was located in a bend of a road under construction at the north base of Stunner Pass.

Ida May was a pleasant, fun loving lady who was always a joy to be around. Always ready for a hike or to go fishing. She was an accomplished fisherwoman who always caught trout. The runoff from an old mine poisoned the creek so we had to hike a half mile or so up the mountain to get beyond the poisoned water in order to fish.

Homer was a tall, full-bodied man who took pride in his walking ability and I believe it bothered him that this kid, his namesake, could keep up with him. It was hard to believe that he was once almost an invalid from tuberculosis. He was dedicated to quality, a hard worker who was bothered by the attitude and work habits of some of the Civilian Conservation Corps workers used in the road construction project. Impatient with the slow progress on one stretch, he pressed me into service one Saturday when the CCC boys were off for the weekend. He ran the Caterpillar tractor dragging the road grader with me taking shouts and gesture instructions as to which wheels to spin to correct blade depth and angle. He was dedicated.

A half mile or so upstream on the Alamosa River from Stunner would be in the vicinity of the Iron Creek confluence with the river, probably Horsethief Park. Wightman Fork joins the Alamosa River about one and a half miles downstream from Stunner and was the source of polluted mine water that poisoned the river. Most of the polluted water came from the Reynolds Tunnel at Summitville that drained into Wightman Fork. In 1934, the fact that natural sources of pollution affected the river above Wightman Fork was not fully understood.

I was a boy scout in Troop 286. Our scoutmaster was Hal Boutwell, a died-in-the-wool prospector. He took me on prospecting trips to the Gold Creek area near Summitville where he had a cabin and several claims. Hal never found the gold he hoped to find but never lost hope that he would. He got me interested in geology and that was one reason why I ended up at the Colorado School of Mines. He showed me bog iron that was precipitated by vegetation along the Alamosa River below Iron Creek in an area he called Government Flats. Vegetation is now commonly used to precipitate metals, particularly iron, from polluted water.

Troop 286 made an unusual entry into the Boy Scout camp at the Beaver Reservoir campground near South Fork when I was fourteen years old. Scoutmaster Boutwell, Dad, and we scouts rode in the back of a Gold Links Mine ore truck from Monte Vista to Summitville The trip took us up the Wightman Fork road from the Alamosa River to Summitville — a real experience. We spent the night in an old building at Summitville and then hiked over North Mountain and down the Beaver Creek drainage to camp - a long, tiring hike of fifteen miles.

Alan Howard, a neighbor when I was growing up, worked in the mines at Summitville and he enjoyed telling me of his experiences underground. He told the story that while at Summitville he was cutting a hitch in a rock wall to set a mine timber and his chisel came up yellow with gold. He said he put mud over the hitch to hide the gold and planned to go back for the gold but never did. He also said that the high-grade ore and mill concentrate was soldered into coffee cans for shipment.

As a teenager I delivered papers to a man who lived in the neighborhood and, according to gossip, had spent time in prison for being a member of a ring that had high-graded gold out of the Summitville mines. The mining company suspected someone in the mine was high-grading gold and hired a security company to infiltrate the mine crew to find out who was involved. The security company agent found out who was involved and thought it was such a good deal that he actually joined the high-graders. In time, the perpetrators were found out and arrested, including the agent. Alan Howard said he knew where some of the high-graded gold was hidden, but was afraid to reclaim it.

A friend of my parents, Mrs. Hanks was a schoolteacher at Summitville. I remember her talking about her experiences there. Some of the children got to school through snow tunnels in the winter months.

I took ROTC at the Colorado School of Mines. Colonel Wendell W. Fertig, who led a guerilla war against the Japanese invasion of the Philippine Islands in World War II, was the professor of military science. He was a mining engineer at a Philippine gold mine at the time of the Japanese invasion. After he graduated from Colorado School of Mines he worked at Summitville for a period of time. He, as a young engineer, was given the job of making time studies of various jobs in the mine.

He told the story of timing a miner using a shovel. The miner finally said that if he, Fertig, was so interested in the damned shovel, he could have it and then he quit and walked out of the mine.

This book is the first comprehensive history of the gold camp called Summitville. Only three histories, to the best of my knowledge, have previously been written about Summitville – Charles W Henderson's *Mining in Colorado*, USGS Professional Paper 138 published in 1926; Thomas A. Steven and James C. Ratte's *Geology and Ore Deposits of the Summitville District, San Juan Mountains, Colorado*, USGS Professional Paper 343 published in 1960; and Ralph C. Ellithorpe's *Poker, Politics and Gold*, published by Denver Westerners, Inc. in their 1971 Brand Book.

I want to acknowledge those who helped me in my effort to document Summitville's history. First, I want to especially thank V. W. "Bill" Ellithorpe, Louise Colville, Arlie Stanger, and Raylene Owen for their most valuable information, memories and pictures.

Bill Ellithorpe's family was much involved in Summitville's history. His father, Harry V. and uncle, Ralph C., the author of *Poker, Politics and Gold,* worked as miners at Summitville in 1928 and 1929. Bill's first trip to Summitville was in 1928 when he was eight years old. He worked there as an underground miner in 1937 and 1941 and he and his brother Bob owned claims in the district. Bill, his son Rick, and Bob built roads and drill pads for the American Smelting & Refining and Anaconda exploration projects in the 1980s. Bob found the Summitville Gold Boulder, now in the Denver Museum of Natural History.

Louise Colville, great-granddaughter of Andrew Edstrom, spent countless hours researching Rio Grande County records and early-day newspapers for information on Summitville for the book. Andrew Edstrom was P. J. Peterson's partner in a planing mill near Del Norte. P. J. Peterson was one of the first discoverers of gold, other than placer gold, at Summitville and one of the important early mine developers. Louise not only researched old records and newspapers but furnished information from P. J. Peterson's personal diary that is in her possession.

Arlie Stanger, who recently celebrated her one-hundredth birthday, lived in Summitville in the 1930s and early 1940s. She taught school at Summitville and her husband, Kenneth, was postmaster at Summitville, the highest post office in the United States. Arlie's memories and pictures of life in Summitville add an important personal and human touch to the book.

Raylene Owen lived with her family as a child in a second story apartment in the Summitville bunkhouse. Her father was the mining company's bookkeeper and payroll clerk. Her memories of Summitville also add a human touch to Summitville's history.

I also wish to thank Monte Vista Historical Society's Peg Schall; Rio Grande County Museum's Nancy Schrader; and Rio Grande Combined Court's Jennifer Martinez for their help. Also Charles Harbert for the use of his Summitville pictures and Dave Bunk for early-day company stock certificates; Mrs. Robert Wardell for allowing me to quote from her father's unpublished transcript, *Ben Poxson, A Reminiscence*; Stanley Dempsey for information about Summitville from his collection of Colorado Mining Association yearbooks; and Intrasearch, Inc. for copies of Summitville aerial photographs. The staffs of the Colorado School of Mines Library and the University of Arizona Main and Science Libraries were very helpful in my research for the book.

Kenneth Paulsen let me have access to his extensive and most helpful information on Summitville, including the Knight Piesold and Company report prepared for the Summitville Study Group in 1993 – a most important source of information on Summitville's latter history.

Phil Bethke, the U.S. Geological Survey's Scientist Emeritus, and my son David, a geologist with Geoscience Australia, reviewed and critiqued the description of the geology of Summitville and the Upper Alamosa River Basin.

Mike Davis of Davis Engineering Service, Alamosa, Colorado, provided me with a Summitville mining claim map that is included as an appendix to the book. Of all the mining and related companies that I worked for during my career, only my first employer, Davis Engineering Service, is still in business.

— Richard C. Huston, Tucson, Arizona

PROLOGUE

Summitville lies in a remote area of the southeastern San Juan Mountains, sometimes called "the Alps of America" because of their rugged mountain peaks, deep canyons, green forests, lush meadows, lakes, and streams. Several of the peaks in the Summitville area, Red Mountain No. 1 and Red Mountain No. 2, have brilliant red and nearly white slopes and can be viewed from the Forest Service observation sign on the Stunner Pass road. This beautiful coloration is caused by the area's unique geology that is described later in the Prologue, as is the area's heavy snowfall during long, cold winters.

Red Mountains No. 1 and 2 from Stunner Pass
Photo by the Author

The Summitville Mining District is between 11,300 and 12,500 feet above sea level, and the upper Alamosa River Basin is not far below. The area is subject to long winters of heavy snowfall and cold temperatures, and short, cool, and rainy summers. As the old timers said: "Don't sleep in on July Fourth because you might miss summer." The Summitville mines are located on the eastern side of South Mountain and the town site is located in the saddle between North and South Mountains along Wightman Fork, a tributary of the Alamosa River. There are no other mining districts in the Summitville area that were nearly as productive as the Summitville mines.

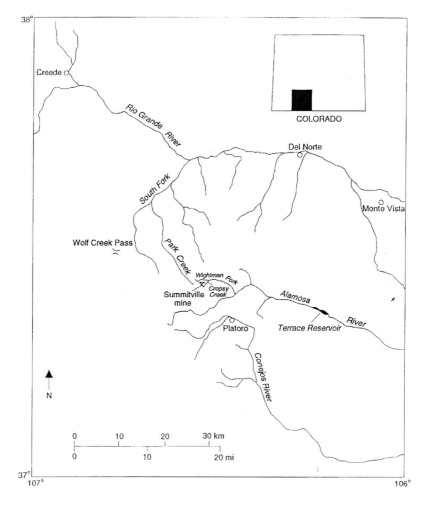

Area Drainage Map
*Environmental Geology of Summitville Mine
by Gray, Coolbaugh, et al*

Summitville and Upper Alamosa River Basin Geology

Many investigations and reports on the geology of Summitville and the upper Alamosa River Basin have been made over the years. The following are only the most comprehensive and descriptive of the area's unusual geologic setting. Many more reports on Summitville geology are available, mostly reports immediately before and after Summitville being made a Superfund Site by the Environmental Protection Agency.

F. M. Endlich, a geologist with the Colorado Hayden Survey, made the first investigation of the Summitville District geology. He visited the Summit District, as Summitville was then known, in June 1875 shortly after its discovery and determined that the gold was associated with limonite, a hydrous iron oxide, an oxidation product of pyrite, iron sulfide.[1] Hayden Survey surveyors arrived in the San Luis Valley in June 1874 and concentrated their work in the San Juan Mountains. They formed a base camp in Del Norte and started to map. They investigated the discovery of valuable minerals at Summit, leading to Endlich's visit and geological investigation. The survey party was affected not only by the high altitude, snow banks and persistent mosquitoes, but by the danger posed by nearby forest fires. As two surveyors, Wilson and Rhoda, were on a peak south of the Summit District, they noticed static electricity in their hair. They retreated down the peak to take cover ahead of the lightning storm, leaving their transit behind. During a break in the storm, Wilson ran back to the summit for the transit and was nearly hit by lightning. The surveyors cautiously got off the peak and into the forest below.[2]

R. C. Hills described the mineralogy of the Summitville District's bonanza gold ores in 1885 in an article in the first volume of Colorado Scientific Society Proceedings entitled *Ore Deposits of Summit District, Rio Grande County, Colorado*.

Horace B. Patton investigated the Summitville District and wrote *Platoro-Summitville Mining District, Colorado*, in Colorado Geological Survey Bulletin 13 in 1917. Thomas A. Steven and James C. Ratte's report, *Geology and Ore Deposits of the Summitville District, San Juan Mountains, Colorado*, U. S.

Geological Professional Paper 343 published in 1960, was the first definitive study of Summitville geology. Thomas A. Steven and Peter W. Lipman described the calderas that formed the San Juan Mountains in U. S. Geological Survey Professional Report 958, *Calderas of the San Juan Volcanic Field, Southwestern Colorado*, published in 1976. Roger Stoffgren described the *Genesis of Acid-Sulfate Alteration and Gold-Copper-Silver Mineralization at Summitville, Colorado* in Economic Geology, Volume 82, in 1987.

The U. S. Geological Survey Bulletin 2220 entitled *Environmental Considerations of Active and Abandoned Mine Lands: Lessons from Summitville*, Trude V. V. King, Editor, was published in 1993. John E. Gray and Mark F. Coolbaugh wrote *Geology and Geochemistry of Summitville, Colorado: An Epithermal Acid Sulfate Deposit in a Volcanic Dome*, Economic Geology, Volume 89, in 1994.

Geology of the Upper Alamosa River Area was described in Rock Talk Volume 4, Number 2, published by the Colorado Geological Survey in 2001. Philip Bethke, Robert O. Rye, Roger E. Stoffregen and Peter G. Vikre were the authors of *Evolution of the Magmatic-Hydrothermal Acid-Sulfate System at Summitville, Colorado: Integration of Geological, Stable-Isotope, and Fluid Inclusion Evidence* published in Chemical Geology in 2005.

The San Juan Mountains are the largest erosion remnant of a volcanic plateau that covered what now is the Southern Rocky Mountains up to a depth of 4,000 feet thirty-five to five million years ago. The San Juans cover an area of about 9,600 square miles and contain about 9,000 cubic miles of lava and other volcanic rocks. The volcanic rocks that mostly make up the rugged San Juan Mountains are geologically young. The geological processes that formed them began about 35 million years ago with the development of scattered strato-volcanoes that were later buried by hot ash clouds or ash-flow sheets. These hot ash clouds or ash-flow sheets spread over the region and formed layers of volcanic rock up to 3,000 feet deep.[3] Volcanic activity occurs when a large body of molten magma is forced up into the earth's crust.

The magma in the magma chamber under the crust is very hot and contains dissolved gases, mostly water vapor under very high pressure. As the magma rises toward the surface, the confining pressure is reduced and the dissolved gases separate from the magma. Since most of the magma that formed the San Juans was very viscous, the gases did not bubble away as in Hawaii but exploded violently and blew the magma into small volcanic ash particles as happened at the Mount St. Helens eruptions. Geologists call the products of such explosive volcanism pyroclastic or "fire broken" rocks. Pyroclastic eruptions force large quantities of volcanic ash into the atmosphere.

The eruption of large volumes of magma to create the San Juan Mountains resulted in the formation of "calderas." Calderas are roughly circular segments of the earth's crust bounded by ring-shaped fractures, or faults, that form when magma is ejected from the magma chamber and leaves a void. The roof over the void collapses, leaving a circular depression at the surface that is the caldera. In many calderas the floors are up-lifted when magmas that created the caldera in the first place are reintroduced into the magma chamber. This forms a resurgent dome. No fewer than seventeen large volume pyroclastic ash flows erupted from the San Juan calderas. About a third of these calderas have economically significant mineralization[4].

The Platoro and Summitville Calderas are the two most easterly of the San Juan calderas and are the dominant geologic features in the upper Alamosa River Basin. The Platoro Caldera began forming about 30 million years ago and is one of the oldest in the San Juans. It had a period of resurgence when lava was re-introduced into the magma chamber and a dome formed within the caldera. Between 29 and 30 million years ago, the eruption of additional ash flows from the Platoro Caldera formed the "nested" Summitville Caldera that is in the northern part of the Platoro Caldera.[5]

Summitville and the upper Alamosa River Basin are located near intersections of the Platoro Caldera ring fractures and the regional Pass Creek-Elwood Creek-Platoro Fault System as shown on the map of the Platoro and Summitville Calderas.[6]

Geologic episodes after the calderas were formed included lava flows and molten igneous rock called stocks that moved upwards from deep within the earth into zones of weakness in the

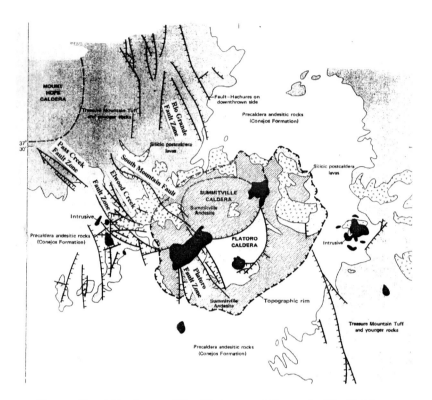

Generalized Geology of the Platoro and Summitville Caldera
*Calderas of the San Juan Volcanic Field, Southwestern Colorado
Steven, Thomas A. and Lipman, Peter W., U. S. G. S. Professional Paper 958,
1976*
(Note: Fault zone names added by author)

earth's crust but cooled and solidified before reaching the surface. A stock is defined as an igneous intrusion with an outcrop of less than forty square miles.

The Alamosa River, Summitville, and Jasper Stocks intruded into the earth's crust around the margins of the Platoro and Summitville Calderas, using the existing caldera ring fractures. These intrusions occurred between 29 and 30 million years ago and the pre-existing faults and fractures were controls that localized the igneous intrusions and resulting hydrothermal activity.[7]

Hydrothermal systems related to the emplacement of the Alamosa River Stock and younger intrusions were responsible for hydrothermal alteration of rock strata in the upper Alamosa

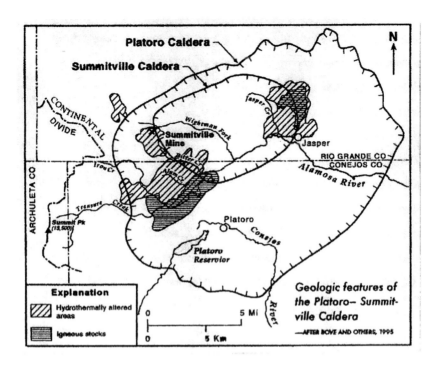

Colorado Geological Survey Special Publication 38, 1995

River basin drainage areas of Iron, Alum, and Bitter Creeks that are upstream of Wightman Fork. The Jasper Stock altered rock in the Jasper and Burnt Creek drainages below Wightman Fork and caused mineralization in the Jasper Mining District. An igneous intrusion, buried about 2,000 feet beneath South Mountain, drove Summitville's rock alteration and mineralization. Opaline and siliceous sinter deposits overlying the igneous stocks in the upper Alamosa River Basin suggest that the area once was similar to Yellowstone Park with a multitude of geysers and hot springs.

Bedrock in the Summitville Mining District, Iron, Alum, and Bitter Creek Basins was extremely attacked by sulfuric acid during hydrothermal alteration. This is known as acid-sulfate alteration. Molten magma beneath the surface contained dissolved gases, mainly sulfur dioxide and hydrogen sulfide, water and metals. As the magma cooled to form the stocks, the gases and water separated taking many metals with them. The gases ascended quickly along faults and fractures. The magmatic gases and water vapor combined chemically to form sulfuric acid. The acid then leached alkalis and, at its most intense, dissolved minerals completely. This process known as acid leaching made the rocks porous. Rocks normally are able to withstand attack by acid solutions by neutralizing the acid. The intensity of acid alteration in the upper Alamosa River Basin and the Summitville Mining District was extreme because these altered rocks no longer had a natural acid neutralizing capacity.[8]

When rocks that contain iron pyrite are exposed the pyrite oxidizes and produces sulfuric acid and iron oxides that stain the surface varying shades of red as dramatically shown on Red Mountains 1 and 2 in the picture on the first page of the Prologue. Natural acid formation and drainage has been active in the upper Alamosa River Basin and Summitville for thousands, perhaps millions of years. The downward cutting action of the streams in the upper Alamosa River Basin exposed the altered rock and led to excessive erosion.

Geologists in the 1950s and 60's determined that the main pollution of the Alamosa River was the leaching of the abundant sulfate minerals formed by the oxidation of pyrite (iron sulfide) in the Alum-Bitter Creek area. The area is laced with sulfates that easily leached out in rainstorms, and the creeks looked milky due to suspended clay minerals formed by the hydrothermal alteration. Newmont and three other exploration companies did limited exploration drilling in the Alum-Bitter Creek area with negative results so far as economic mineralization. One cloudburst in the 1950s swept a Newmont Mining Company drill down a steep gully and apparently into the Alamosa River. It was never found.[9] Alum Creek was obviously named "alum" after the chemical compound, hydrated potassium aluminum sulfate, that occurs naturally along Alum and Bitter Creeks and their tributaries.

Alunite is commonly formed by acid sulfate alteration of volcanic rocks and was first mentioned by Endlich as being in the Summitville area. Alunized rocks are most abundant in a zone of alteration near Lookout Muntain.[10]

The U. S. Forest Service sign at the Stunner Pass Overview looking north across the Alamosa River toward Red Mountains reads as follows:

The mountains you see before you are rich in iron and other metals. Unvegetated slopes are highly erodable and provide a continuous supply of acidity and heavy metals into the Alamosa River. Many springs discharging from these mountains are naturally acidic and can contain more heavy metals than mine discharge in this area. Metal contributions from these mountains have occurred for thousands of years. Natural acidity, coupled with human caused activity, results in the river conditions you see today.

A nail left in Alum Creek will soon disappear. This nail would break down in the natural acidic conditions of Alum Creek in about eight months.

Magmatic fluids given off by the igneous intrusion buried beneath South Mountain, caused the alteration and mineralization at Summitville. The violent eruption of Washington State's Mount St. Helens in 1980 was accompanied by the growth of a volcanic dome made by the eruption of molten lava. The formation of the Summitville volcanic dome is similar to that at Mount St. Helens. It was made of an igneous rock called quartz-latite. As previously described, the magmatic gases and water vapor poured through the dome and created porosity. Acid leaching resulted in openings, called vugs, in the surrounding rock that were filled with quartz crystals.

The vuggy silica and quartz-alunite alterations provided openings, or "plumbing" that allowed hydrothermal solutions emanating from the igneous stock below as it cooled to permeate the rock. These solutions deposited the gold and sulfide minerals at Summitville. The gold and sulfide mineralization came after the formation of the vuggy silica alteration and was not directly related to the highly acidic solutions required to create the original openings.[11]

The ore veins at Summitville are normally short; however, one is over 1,600 feet long. Mineralization in the veins extended vertically for about 1,000 feet and some ore shoots were 30 feet wide. The primary mineralization occurred in veins and fracture-controlled silicified ledges. Secondary high-grade gold ore occurred in vertical pipes and at the intersections of fractures. The gold content in the upper oxidized zone of 300 feet, more or less, was enriched. The ore below the oxidized zone contained less gold and sulfide minerals, primarily of copper- enargite, covellite, chalcocite, and chalcopyrite – and small amounts of sphalerite and galena.[12]

Faults, fractures, and joints in the altered Summitville volcanic dome allowed the hydrothermal fluids to react with a large volume of rock, precipitating gold in small amounts over a wide area, thus resulting in a large, low-grade gold deposit in addition to the high-grade vein-like structures and pods mined by underground mining methods.[13] The open pit indicated on the following plan view and mining of this large low-grade deposit is discussed in Chapter Six.

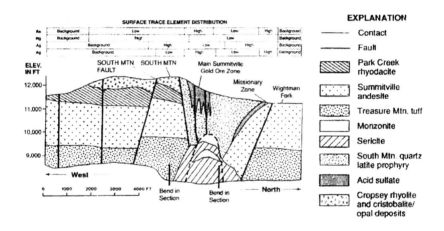

Schematic Cross-Section of the Summitville District
Modified from Steven and Ratte' (1960) and Enders and Coolbaugh (1987)

Weather

The San Juan Mountains are known for long winters with heavy snow and cool wet summers. Summitville and the upper Alamosa River Basin are located just east of the Continental Divide between Wolf Creek Pass to the west and Cumbres Pass to the south where winter snows are heavy even by San Juan standards. The mountain peaks along the Continental Divide

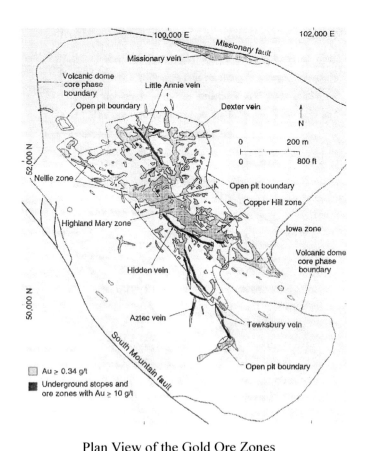

Plan View of the Gold Ore Zones
Gray, J. E. and Coolbaugh, Mark F., Economic Geology, Volume 89, 1994

seem to catch the winter storm clouds and hold them while they drop great amounts of snow.

    Wolf Creek Pass, fifty miles north of Cumbres Pass, is well known for its heavy snowfall, avalanches, and superb skiing. The Summitville area snowfall averages about 400 inches in the winter and thunderstorms are common during the summer months. Total annual precipitation averages fifty-five inches, mostly as snowfall, and the annual evaporation rate is about twenty-four inches. Temperatures in the winter vary from forty to minus-fifteen degrees Fahrenheit. Summer temperatures vary from seventeen to seventy degrees Fahrenheit.[14]

Cumbres Pass had very heavy snowfall in the winter of 1883-1884. The railroad crossing Cumbres Pass was blocked by snow from mid-November, 1883 until mid- to late June 1884. In March 1884, W. D. Carroll, a telegraph operator in Alamosa, was sent out with a snow-bucking crew of 200 men and four engines whose job was to clear snow from the railroad tracks. Carroll's job was to check the telegraph line. He described the snow depths along the railway:

Our first stop was at Big Horn siding, twenty miles from Antonito. I did not need pole climbers as I could walk out anywhere on top of the snow and tap the wires. As the telegraph poles were about twenty feet high you can have some idea of the depth of the snow. As we progressed toward the summit, the snow became deeper until it reached a depth of thirty-five to forty feet.[15]

Summitville was severely impacted by the heavy winter snow, particularly in the early days before snow plowing equipment was available. Skis and snowshoes were the only modes of transportation available in the winter for many years. Mail was delivered to Summitville by snowshoe three days during the week. If the mail carrier could carry more than the weight of the mail, he would bring square cut nails or charcoal needed by the mines. He was paid fifty cents a pound for his effort.[16]

The first heavy snow of the winter of 1885-1886 blocked the road from Summitville. Horses owned by a freighter named Brockman were scheduled to leave camp but couldn't because of the heavy snow. They were kept at Summitville until mid-March, when they traveled to the low country on snowshoes! The snowshoes were made of wood planks, two inches thick, eight inches wide and eighteen inches long and were fastened to the horses' hooves by wires and straps. After days of practice, the horses learned how to maneuver on their most unusual snowshoes. Brockman rode one horse over fifty feet of snow, while the other horses followed pulling a sled of provisions. Brockman and his horses left Summitville at 9 a.m. on a March Monday and were past the deep snow by 5 p.m. that night. What a story![17]

Welch Nossaman was born in Pella, Iowa in 1851. He helped bring a mill out to Colorado for Dr. B. F. Keebies, who followed the gold rush to Del Norte. He then pioneered in the

San Juan Mountains in the 1870s. Nossaman hauled lumber, supplies, and the mail to Summitville and then gold bullion from Summitville to Del Norte. One winter he also helped people get out of the mountains.[18]

This is his story somewhat abridged. To save expenses when he had the mail contract from Summitville to Del Norte, Nossaman let one of the men who was helping him go and took one shift himself on snowshoes. From Del Norte to Summitville was twenty-eight miles, and he rode up to the toll house on a horse and from there to Summitville on snowshoes. He would stay all night at Summitville and then come back to Del Norte, first by snowshoes and then by horse.

Nossaman got into Summitville one night after dark. There was about two feet of fresh snow and it was still snowing very hard. After he got there with the mail, several folks came in and wanted to know if he thought they and their families could get out.

Sam Sibbetts had three or four yoke of cattle and Nossaman believed that the cattle could plow through the snow because it was soft. The families could then follow with their buggies and freight wagons and get out all right.

The group got ready at night, so they could start at daylight because it would be hard going for the first five or six miles. Jack Burris took his mining crew of fifteen or twenty men to shovel the big drifts so the oxen could get through and then be followed by the rest of the party.

Nossaman stayed in Summitville until it was time to leave with the mail (about 8 or 9 a.m.) and then caught up with the party on top of the hill. It was still very stormy and the men were all bunched up and the wind was howling. Nossaman asked Roof Bloise, Jack Burris' foreman, what was going on. Roof said they had shut the mine down and were pulling out. The men in the mine crew had given up getting out of the mountains because of the deep snow and strong wind. Nossaman asked about the cattle's location and was told they were over the divide in a little basin and covered by snow. Some of the men helped Nossaman get the cattle out single file on their way to the toll house. Burris and his horses then followed the trail left by the cattle before the snow filled the trail again. The women rode the horses and the men rode the mules or hiked behind them to the tollhouse. Buggies and freight wagons were left behind until after the storm passed.

After the party arrived at the tollhouse and built a roaring fire in the fireplace, Mrs. Trelore missed her six-month old baby. She said she didn't bring the baby out but gave it to Mr. Hoover. Mr. Hoover said he "throwed it up front of Joe Simmons on a mule in a roll of bedding." Simmons said he dumped the bedding a mile or two above the toll house. Nossaman got on his snowshoes and walked back along the trail until he found the roll of bedding. In it was the baby, dry and not crying. He brought it back to the toll house and its mother, who then asked where was her little poodle. No one knew. The next day the men went up to get the wagons and found the dog covered with snow but it was all right.[19]

Snow slides or avalanches were a hazard at Summitville. Schinzel Flats, at the headwaters of Iron Creek was named for two brothers who died in an avalanche while prospecting.[20] At another time, brothers Ralph and Harry Ellithorpe and Gunny Lewis had a lease on a mining property on South Mountain and built a shack over their shaft for convenience. However, an avalanche wrecked their shack and buried their tools. They decided to give up mining on that property.[21]

The average annual snowfall at Summitville is thirty-five to forty feet. Roads are kept open to the outside world today by a bulldozer working eight to sixteen hours a day during the winter months.[22]

Arlie Stanger whose husband Kenneth was the postmaster at Summitville from 1938 to 1942 tells this story about an unsuccessful trip to Summitville during the winter:

Getting to camp from the valley could be a challenge. Although the company kept the road plowed, a snowstorm could make it very slick. On Friday evening, Kenny and I started up. When we got to the switchbacks (the Wightman Fork road) outside of camp we were in trouble. Those last six miles of narrow road wound up a steep incline. We hit a very slick spot and couldn't make it over the top in spite of chains and a shovel. Kenny would make it almost over that ridge and we'd start to slide back. He would back down the narrow road – straight up one side and straight down on the other – but we were too interested on making it to be afraid. Finally we had to give up and head back to Monte Vista only to get stuck in a barrow pit on level ground. It had snowed so much while we were on the hill that the road disappeared. We finally made it back to Monte Vista just as the sun came up. We used to joke that there were only two seasons at the camp – winter and the Fourth of July. [23]

Tom Bond III, a geologist who spent the summer and fall of 1969 working at Summitville, made the following comments about snow at Summitville:

The summer I worked at Summitville was very wet. Access for most of the summer was the Park Creek road. We were not able to use the shorter Piños Creek road from Del Norte until July due to an 80 foot deep snow bank on the north side of Old Baldy. The Park Creek road was closed by snow to all but four-wheel vehicles for a few days in July. In October we often had to use two Caterpillar tractors and a patrol grader to keep the last two miles of the road open. One day, coming down the hill on snow, our Jeep did a 450 degree spin. When it stopped there was nothing but sky in the windshield and the front wheels were about six inches from going over the edge. [24]

Herb Stanger on snow bank above the Summitville Road
Courtesy of Arlie Stanger

CHAPTER 1
DISCOVERY
1870 -1874

Gold was first discovered at the headwaters of Wightman Fork in the summer of 1870. Summitville was established and became one of the earliest and most successful mining camps in southwestern Colorado. The prospector's gold pan was the tool that located and produced the first placer gold. The first prospectors followed the trail of placer gold up Wightman Fork and discovered its source, rich gold deposits on South Mountain. Very little is known about the first discoverers. Short biographies of two of them are included, as well as an early history of the town of Del Norte that is related to Summitville.

In his report for 1875, R. W. Raymond gives a summary of the mining developments in Rio Grande County for 1870 through 1874 as follows[1]:

The first discovery of gold in the Summit district was made in Wightman's Gulch about the last of June 1870, by a party consisting of James L. Wightman, E. Baker, J. Carey French, Sylvester Reese, and William Boran, Wightman getting the first "prospect." All of the party, with the exception of Wightman and Reese left by the middle of September. Wightman and Reese engaged in sluicing, until the 9th of November, when they left, heavily packed, and made their way out through snow waist deep, reaching the Rio Grande in three days.

In the spring of 1871, a large number of people flocked into the Summit, hundreds arriving while the snow was yet very deep and work impracticable. A general disgust soon took possession of the prospectors and by the end of August there were but three men in the district — J. L. Wightman, P. J. Peterson and J. P. Johnson. These then remained until about the 20th of October. Wightman and Peterson being the last to leave. They took the gold realized by sluicing to Denver and had it refined at the mint, dividing $170 between the three after paying all expenses of the season's operations; not a very encouraging yield for a hard summer's work. Several lodes had in the meantime been found, or at least lode locations made. The specimens found in the gulch indicated to the miners that they had not washed far, and they believed the parent ledges in place were close by.

In 1872 a few locations were made, and 1873 witnessed a new immigration into the district, and in that year the richest mines in the Summit district were located. The Esmond and Summit lodes were staked during the summer and on September 13th, F. H. Brandt and P. J. Peterson located the Little Annie, Del Norte and Margaretta mines. During 1874 a vast number of new locations were made.

The first five discoverers of the Summitville gold camp, as reported by Raymond, were Union Army veterans of the Civil War who called Topeka, Kansas home. They called themselves the O.K. Company.[2] The O.K. Company met in Santa Fe and had originally planned to prospect in the San Juan Mountains near Baker's Park near Silverton in 1868, but were turned away by the Ute Indians who claimed the land prior to the 1873 Brunot Treaty with the United States.

The five returned to Santa Fe, but, in the spring of 1870 traveled back to the mountains where they followed the South Fork of the Rio Grande to Park Creek. They then traveled up Park Creek to a mountain stream running along the base of 13,000-foot South Mountain, naming it Wightman Fork. Here they camped and stayed for the summer, prospecting along the Wightman Fork. Encouraged by finding a few gold nuggets, they returned the following spring of 1871, built a cabin along Wightman Fork with bedsteads, a table, and a door. Occasional trips were made to La Loma, near the future Del Norte, for supplies. P. J. Peterson had joined the O.K. Company during the previous winter.

J. Cary French went to La Loma, the little Hispanic settlement on the hillside on San Francisco Creek where the Del

Norte High School now stands. French's friend, Juanita Valdez, lived in this area, now unofficially called Sleepytown by local residents.[3] French then traveled north to Saguache with his pony and burros for lumber to build sluices to recover placer gold, but he found none. Then he traveled to the Conejos sawmill where he found the lumber he wanted and his burros hauled it back to Wightman Fork.

Sluicing for gold, prospecting, and filing claims at the Conejos County Courthouse continued all summer. A mining district was formed and named "Summit." It was renamed "Summitville" in 1880, with Wightman as its recorder. About 150 prospectors and miners were in the district during 1871 and were engaged in prospecting and placer mining. Many placer claims were located along Wightman Fork, extending nearly seven miles down stream. P. J. Peterson and F. H. Brandt both filed placer claims for twenty acres each on September 17, 1873.[4]

It was obvious to the prospectors that the gold in the placers was originally deposited in nearby mineralized veins before being eroded and washed down to Wightman Fork. The prospectors swarmed over the slopes of South Mountain looking for outcrops of veins that carried the gold. This was a slow, tedious, and backbreaking process. Those prospectors fortunate enough to find an outcrop staked a lode claim over their discovery.

Other than perhaps the Frenchmen of Treasure Mountain and Spanish explorers, the first discoverer of a gold lode deposit at Summitville was probably John Esmond, who owned a ranch near Conejos. His discovery was made in 1870 when he found a ledge with free gold under unusual circumstances. His neighbor's daughter, with another girl, ran away to the mountains. Esmond and the neighbor girl's brother looked for the two runaways the next day and found their horses in a meadow near what is now Summitville. As he searched for the girls, he found a gold deposit.[5]

He mined fifty pounds of specimens that were very rich with gold and made four claims at the location of his discovery in the Summit area. However Esmond did no assessment work to hold his right to the claims as required by the Mining Act of 1872. That act gave prospectors the right to file claims on mineral deposits they discovered on public lands, but the discoverer had to perform annual assessment work and record it in the county courthouse in order maintain his right of ownership.

Esmond went to the Summit area in the spring of 1873, intending to work his prospects. To his amazement a cabin was being built at the site; horses and burros were grazing; and two busy men were digging away at the very place he had made his locations. The busy men seen by Esmond were P. J. Peterson and Ferdinand H. Brandt. They had located three lode claims at the site of Esmond's discovery. These claims were the Little Annie, Del Norte, and Margaretta, three of the district's most prolific gold producers. The Little Annie claim was named after Peterson's daughter. Esmond then located the Esmond (later called the Aztec) and Major lode claims nearby as a consolation. The claims were made in accordance with the Mining Act of 1872 and the laws of the Summit Mining District. The claim notices were originally filed in Conejos County prior to the organization of Rio Grande County, which included Summitville within its boundaries. The claims were then certified to Rio Grande County in 1874.[6]

On July 31, 1873, Peterson located the Del Norte lode. Thomas Keyes located the Margaretta claim on September 10, 1873, and shortly thereafter conveyed his interest in the claim to Peterson and Brandt. The Margaretta claim was likely named after Brandt's sister-in-law. Dr. R. F. Adams purchased the Esmond (Aztec) claim, where rich gold ore was discovered by Theodore Goupil in 1872.[7]

Late in the afternoon of September 13, 1873, Peterson and his partner Brandt found a very rich gold vein outcrop. Brandt's attention was attracted by the glitter of pure gold lying at his feet. P. J. Peterson was only a few yards away at the time of the discovery, and both were credited with finding the Little Annie lode.[8] According to Rio Grande County records, P. J. Peterson located the Little Annie and Del Norte claims and then sold one-half of them to F. H. Brandt.[9]

On October 8, 1873, Peterson and Brandt sold the Little Annie, Del Norte, and Margaretta lode claims and two placer claims to a group of investors represented by Charles Adam for $500,000, with $410,000 paid to Peterson and Brandt.[10] A corporation was formed with Peterson and Brandt having the controlling interest in the mine.

Charles Adams, a German who changed his name from Karl Adam Schwanbeck, held the rank of general in the Colorado Militia and saw service in the Civil War. He was in charge of the Ute Agency at Los Piños from 1872 to 1874. He was a friend of Chief Ouray and helped gain the release of captive women after the Meeker Massacre.[11]

The *Colorado Daily Pueblo Chieftain*, Pueblo, Colorado reported in its October 10, 1873 issue: *The Little Annie gold mine, located near the San Juan Mining District in Conejos County, was yesterday sold by Messrs. Peterson and Brandt, original owners, through the agency of Crone and Hahn in this city for $410,000.* Colonel Gillette staked the Little Ida claim in July 1874. The Golden Queen claim was located in late September 1873 by Josiah Mann, O. P. Posey, John Grant and others.

A large number of claims were staked in 1874 bringing the total of claims filed to about 2,500. Only about a dozen of all these claims would prove to be valuable. The attention of mine owners then turned to getting machinery to Summitville for reducing the ores and recovering gold.

Unfortunately very little is known about the lives of the Summitville discoverers. What is known follows:

Pear Joshua Peterson[12]

Pear J. Peterson was born in Sandsjo Socken, Sweden, on February 28, 1838. He migrated to the United States with his parents in 1852 and they then went to Chicago. In the summer of 1852, he first went to Kansas then to Missouri. He returned to Chicago in 1861. He was back in Lawrence, Kansas in 1863. He assisted in the reconstruction of Lawrence after the Quantrell raid and served as an orderly sergeant in Company B, Third Kansas Regiment.

He left Lawrence in 1868 and went to Dickinson County, Kansas and then to Fort Wallace. In 1867 he married Lavina Hickey and she gave birth to twins, Annie Charlotta and Wallace John, in 1869. In the fall of 1869, he returned with his family to

Lawrence, Kansas. Another daughter, Jenny Catherina was born in 1870.

Peterson heard of the gold strike at Summitville and headed there in the spring of 1871. By 1874 the Peterson family was living in Del Norte in a log cabin at the site of the present Windsor Hotel. Mrs. Peterson was active in the Del Norte business world, buying property and running a small restaurant for a short time. Mrs. Peterson died in February 1875 shortly after giving birth to stillborn twins, Frank and Florence. She and her twins are buried in the Del Norte Cemetery in graves no longer marked.

Peterson continued to work at the Little Annie Mine in 1875, leaving about Christmas time to take his three children back to Kansas. While they were in Del Norte, Peterson's children were taken care of by his planing mill business partners' wives, Mrs. Edstrom and Mrs. Olson. Peterson also boarded with the Edstroms. He would travel back to Lawrence during the winters to spend time with his children.

On one of these trips he met Britta Mary Anderson and fell in love. He married her, and on April 11, 1877 wrote in his diary that "today is one of the greatest days of my life, my wedding day." P. J. and Mary lived in Del Norte for a time and then moved to the Summit mining camp. They returned to Lawrence on a regular basis to visit family and friends and had three sons, Albert, George and Fred.

Peterson and Brandt sold their shares in the Little Annie Mine to New York interests in February 1880 for $50,000. The Petersons were then living on the farm he purchased northwest of Lawrence, Kansas. In July 1880, Peterson returned to Del Norte to sell his share of the Peterson and Edstrom planing mill in Del Norte. He also visited friends in the Swedish Colony north of present-day Monte Vista known as Swede Lane.

P. J. Peterson died on March 26, 1906 after a paralytic stroke at the age of 68. His son, Albert, died the following August.

J. Carey French

In August 1871, J. Carey French took twenty-five pounds of ore and six ounces of Summitville gold dust to be assayed at the Denver Mint. It was said to be the finest bar ever brought to the mint. News spread like wildfire, and the flood of prospectors and miners began.[13]

J. Carey French was a major in the Union Army who served with distinction in the 2nd Kansas Cavalry, and he was Adjutant-General on the staff of General Blunt during the noted campaign of 1862-1863 in northwestern Arkansas and the Indian Nation. After the Civil War he was appointed by President Grant as agent to the Navajo Indians at Abiqui, New Mexico. He was an active member of the Grand Army of the Republic.[14] He purchased 160 acres of land to develop the town site of Del Norte in 1872.[15] In the winter of 1873, he sent for his wife and children who met him in Denver and then traveled to their new home in Del Norte.[16] French managed the Shaw Springs hotel and spring for several years in his later life.[17]

French's obituary in the *Del Norte Prospector* follows[18]:

Major J. Carey French, one of the oldest pioneers of the Valley, died at his home in Del Norte, Friday night, October 18, 1889. The funeral took place at 10 o'clock a.m. under the auspices of the Masonic Fraternity and the Grand Army of the Republic Post. The funeral is said to have been one of the largest ever held in Del Norte. Major J. Carey French was one of the leading spirits of the Baker's exploring party that wintered where Silverton now stands, in the early days of the "San Juan country."

J. Carey French kept a diary of his activities in 1872 that were transcribed from the original by Arthur C. French, J. Carey's son, in October 1936 as follows[19]:

<u>Tuesday, May 23</u> - *Left Topeka at 2:30 AM. Bought ticket to Denver $39.00. Manhattan at sunrise. Breakfast at Salina. Supper at Wallace. Took sleeping berth with Jack, $2.00.*

<u>Wednesday, May 24</u> - *Arrived in Denver at 7:00AM. Went to Broadworld House. Met Jesus Martinez and Juan de la Cruz from Loma.*

<u>Thursday, May 25</u> - *No entry.*

<u>Friday, May 26</u> - *Got my boots from Topeka via Wells Fargo & Co's Express. Bought groceries of Wm. Cowell. Visited the Mint. Sold some gold at $16.38 per ounce. Met Mr. J. S. Fuller from Loma. Heard that everything was lively. Loaded up after noon. Met Cap't Hawks. Left town at 6:30, camped about a mile*

out. Names of party - J. H. Hunter, Forest Hill, Kans. Johnson, Emporia, Kans. Peterson, Abaline, Ks.

<u>Wednesday, June 7</u> - Broke camp at 6 AM. 12 miles to Loma, north side of Rio Grande, which we made at half past ten. Crossed baggage, tools in a small ferry boat. Very dangerous crossing. Could not cross the mules and wagon. Went up to Juanita's. Met old friends and acquaintances. Returned to camp on the river bank after dark.

<u>Thursday, June 8</u> - Cold night, but pleasant this morning. Moved our camp to the home of Juanita Valdez. John came over the river. Met Mr. and Mrs. Lorain and am going to start to the mines tomorrow with a few supplies.

<u>Friday, June 9</u> - Packed two burros and took Robin and started at 6:30. Camped for dinner 14 miles up the cañon at 12. Left camp at 2. Rough road this afternoon, made 6 miles and camped at 6:30. Cap. Davis, Miller and Dr. ___ came in at 7 o'clock, walked nearly all day. Sat up till 11 o'clock. Wore the skin off my right foot.

<u>Saturday, June 10</u> - Called the camp at 4 o'clock, got breakfast at 5. Burros gone and Sam out hunting them. Returned at 7:30 and packed up and left. Passed the Beaver Dam at 9. Road steep and rough, with quantities of fallen timber and mud and snow. Dinner and rest 2 hours all but Sam Lauren. Tired nearly out. At half past one broke camp, gained the summit about 3. Got into camp a little past 10 tired out, met Wightman, Dewey, Reese and others. Pitched tent on Baker's Hill.

<u>Sunday, June 11</u> - Got up late. Pleasant and warm this morning. After dinner went up the creek to look at my claims. Found everything all right. Rain afternoon.

<u>Monday, June 12</u> - Commenced cutting and laying logs for a house.

<u>Thursday, June 15</u> - Finished the roof, built fireplace and daubed part of the house. Built bedsteads and moved in. Rain in PM.

<u>Friday, June 16</u> - Peterson, Johnson and I commenced work in the gulch. Opened waste ditch, set head gates, built dam this forenoon. Afternoon commenced ditch for the sluice boxes. Worked in water nearly all day. Tired at night.

Saturday, June 17 - Peterson, Johnson and self went up to work at 7 o'clock. Completed dam and ground sluices and ditch for the boxes. Pleasant all day.

Monday, June 19 - Worked on claim today PM. Set boxes and ground sluiced some.

Thursday, June 22 - Cleaned up the pit and the sluices. Anniversary of the discovery of the gulch. Wightman, Dewey and all hands feeling pretty blue.

Friday, June 13 - Up at Sunrise. Started for Loma about half past 7 in company with Cap't Davis, Dr. Chard, Reese, Davis and another Mexican.

Saturday, June 24 - Very cold night, froze ½ inch. Got to Juanita's about half past ten. Changed clothes and went down to the Plaza to the celebration o' la dia San Juan. Big race for the chicken and a fandango.

Friday, June 30 - Up and off at 6 AM. Took the lead up the mountain. On the divide bore SW and came down Reese's gulch, home at ten AM. Found the boys all well and glad to see me or the grub. Royal's party all quit work and came to camp for tobacco, they had been out for three days.

Saturday, July 1 - Saw $54.00 nugget which the Frenchman and Theodore took out on a sluice fork also quite an amount of other specimens. Commenced with Dewey, Reese, Johnson and Peterson on Dewey's "Forlorn Hope" on "Wightman's Folly" 12 x 8. Sunk 7 feet, sent over to make bargain with Scott and Fred to work 3 or 4 claims.

Sunday, July 2 - Reese brought in from Emmet's gulch a burro supposed to belong to a Mr. McNutt a young man from New York who left here two weeks ago alone on a hunt. As he expected to be absent only a few days we fear some accident has befallen him.

Monday, July 3 - Wightman went above on his upper creek claim to work.

Tuesday, July 4 - Peterson and Johnson fired a salute with their revolvers. All went to work on Forlorn Hope. Snow and hail this forenoon. Last day on the Forlorn Hope.

Wednesday, July 5 - Opened Wightman's old prospect hole, worked til night, 18 foot and bed-rock, no prospect. Took tools home. Gave a pair of boots to McNutt who was barefoot and sore from his long siege in the mountains. He left for below.

Tuesday, July 11 - Cleaning up bed-rock. Worked down at the pit. Cleaned up boxes afternoon. Got 23 dols.

Monday, July 17 - Worked down at claim today, pleasant, cleaning bed-rock.

Wednesday, July 19 - Expect to get cleaned up today. Scottie found another nugget, weighs 8 3/4 dwts. Afternoon, big showers came up at 2 o'clock, all hands came to the house from Wightman's and Swedes claims.

Thursday, July 20 - Finished cleaning up 61 ½ dwts.

Tuesday, July 25 - Rough bedrock. Do not expect much from this pit.

Wednesday, July 26 - Cleaned up today. Got 23 dwts.

Sunday, July 30 - Scottie went over the haunts south and brought in some specimens of ore which I am certain is tin or very much resembles the ore which Bill took to Denver last winter. We concluded to go prospecting for the lead tomorrow.

Monday, July 31 - This morning Fred, Scottie and I took pick shovel and gun and started out across the mountain. Pretty hard walk for about 4 miles brought us to where we found the lead or strong indications. Opened a hole below a ledge of ore and took out some nice specimens which we brought home.

Wednesday, August 2 - Left at 7:30 with Fred, Royal and Johnson with four pack animals for Loma. Walked over the divide, found indications of several leads. Found good ore. Camped for dinner at Beaver Dam. 23 miles today.

Thursday, August 3 - Got to Loma about half past nine. Mexicans all out carrying Saint Guadalupe from house to house with drum, fiddle, guitar and great noise.

Saturday, August 5 - Rode to Saguache, about 34 miles by 8 o'clock.

Saturday, August 12 - About half past seven or eight we shouldered the saddle bags containing about 25 pounds of ore, my traveling bag and coats and pulled out afoot.

Monday, August 14 - Called on Mr. Davis to ascertain if a private assayer could be found. Also went to the Mint and met Jas. Pattersch. Afternoon had a talk with him. He advised going to Central, got address of Prof. Hall and concluded to start on morning train.

<u>Tuesday, August 15</u> - At 7:30 took cars for Golden with about five pounds ore on my way to Central.. At Golden got into a 6 horse coach, 9 inside and 5 outside passengers. Slow traveling but fast company, two fortune telling women, two brutish drunken Irishmen, two ladies, a Dutchman, a Nebraska Patent Right man and myself. Got to Black hawk about half past four.

<u>Wednesday, August 16</u> - Went down to Prof. Hill's office at 9 o'clock. Could not get my assay made by him today. After dinner, Prof. Hill called at my hotel and directed me to Dr. Van Shults, Central, where I went. The ore I showed him was manganese of iron.

<u>Thursday, August 17</u> - Left Blackhawk at 9:30 on the coach for Golden City.

<u>Friday, August 18</u> - Took to the U.S. branch Mint this morning 10 15/100 oz. of gold dust to be melted, assayed and stamped.

<u>Saturday, August 19</u> - Directed to call at 10 o'clock for my bar of gold. At 2 o'clock got from the mint an 8 ounce bar, value $162.88 being 984,1000 fine and 14 silver said to be the finest bar every brought to this mint.

<u>Friday, September 1</u> - Saddled up and started for the mines at about 8. In attempting to cross the "Piños" higher, I lost nearly an hour. Got to point of rocks at 12. At 4:30 run into camp of Fred and Scottie and Theodore and the Frenchman on their way out, having quit work and abandoned the mines.

<u>Saturday, September 2</u> - Broke camp at 7:30. Got to Hog Back at 11:30 and to camp about 2. Found Wightman, Johnson and Peterson at work. Went to my old cabin on Baker's Hill.

<u>Sunday, September 3</u> - With Wightman started for "Tinapolis." Spent some hours among the rocks of South Mountain. Brought tools from claims and followed the top of the mountain back. Reese called and found my appointment as judge of election and board of registry for Precinct No. 8 for the election on the 12th.

<u>Tuesday, September 5</u> - Went up to the volcanic iron spring, prospected 3 pans of dirt on cement bench, pretty good colors.

Thursday, September 7 - *Packed up, bid good bye to Wightman's Fork and rolled out. Very cold on the range. Made about 8 or 9 miles in a rainstorm and camped. It soon cleared up a little and we made our beds under a big spruce tree and turned in.*

Tuesday, September 12 - *Opened polls at 8 o'clock. 30 votes cast at noon. As all had voted, adjourned to the store. All hands "spliced the main brace" and had a jolly time.*

Wednesday, October 18 - *John Gredig made me a quit claim deed to 40 acres of land, found corners and took up 160 acres for a town site.*

Thursday, October 19 - *Drew a town plot and went down to Richardson's. Paced off the ground between John's ranch and Richardson. Wightman got in today.*

Friday, October 20 - *Wightman stopped with me last night. Tried to settle lines between our claims. Failed to do so and after sharp talking, concluded to drop the concern and start again.*

Monday, October 23 - *Went to town site - laying out lots and blocks. Named the new town "Del Norte."*

Del Norte

Del Norte was known as the "gateway to the San Juans" because of the large number of people and freight that passed through the town. The first United States Land Office was established in Del Norte in 1875 to protect the rights of the miners as defined in the Mining Act passed by Congress in 1872.

When the first land office officials reached Del Norte they were so disappointed that they, except for John Cleghorn, returned to Iowa stating that "the whole country was infested with rattlesnakes, prairie wolves and Indians." They did report, however, that placer gold was being mined on a high, bald mountain southwest of Del Norte.[20]

John Cleghorn was the first registrar. He remained registrar until his death on December 20, 1880. His son, John, was the land office registrar for six years after his father's death.[21]

When Rio Grande County was formed in 1874, Del Norte was designated the county seat and had a population of about 1,500.

CHAPTER 2
BONANZA
1875-1887

Summitville's short-lived bonanza began in 1875 when amalgamation, a process using mercury, was used to recover gold from the Summitville ore. It ended in 1887 when amalgamation of ores deeper in the ore body containing sulfide minerals recovered only a small portion of the gold that was in the ore and was not economical. Between 1875 and 1887 the district produced almost 94,000 troy ounces of gold and 107,000 troy ounces of silver for a value of more than $2 million in then existing metal prices. By 1883 Summitville was the third largest gold producer in Colorado.

In this chapter the mines and mills are described as well as the mining companies that were organized. Tom Bowen's biography is included as is a description of life and times during the bonanza period. The chapter ends with a description of a stagecoach holdup and an attempted gold theft on the day Summitville mining was shut down.

In his reports for 1875 and 1876, Raymond gives a summary of the beginning of Summitville's bonanza.[1]

The chief gold-producing property of Summit district, and of the territory known as the San Juan mining region, is owned by the Little Annie Mining Co. and comprises the Little Annie, Del Norte, and Margaretta gold mines, and two placer claims of 20 acres each, situated in the gulch below them, with a 10-stamp mill, business and assay office, store, bunkhouse, mess house, retor house, charcoal house, blacksmith shop, tramway, substantial mine and mill dumps, dam, flumes, sluices, etc.

South Mountain – Summit District
Photo by J. J. Cornish, Del Norte, circa 1881-1889
Courtesy of the Rio Grande County Museum, Del Norte, Colorado

The ores of the Del Norte and Margaretta mines have not yet been tested in the mill. Average assay value of former, $43.37; of latter, $24.29. The Del Norte has yielded exceedingly rich pan prospects, and on the 26th of August 1876, a very rich deposit of flour gold was found on the Margaretta, the extent of which has not been determined.

The Little Annie has had more development than any mine in the district, some 1,200 tons of ore having been taken out, but it is as yet only an open quarry. Specimens have been assayed all the way from $70 to $16,000 per ton at the Denver Mint and elsewhere. The average value of the ore is best shown by the result of last autumn's (1875) millwork in which 306 tons taken from the face of the mine, without any sorting, yielded $31,444 or $102.68 per ton. The gold is chiefly in the form of "flour" and for the most part invisible, although fine specimens are occasionally taken, some being of a very large size. The fineness of the retorts has been about 980, as shown by certificates from the mint at Denver and from the United States assay office at New York.

The Little Annie Mill has at present but 10 stamps, but there are 64 stamps working under contract on Annie ore at a cost to the company of $10 per ton. The product of its own mill (at the average so far of $3,000 per week) is $156,000 per annum.

The placers have been worked only at intervals, without system and without machinery. In this mode they have yielded some very fine nuggets.

The Golden Star Gold & Silver Mining Co. owns three mines and has erected a mill on Wightman Fork with ten stamps and provisions for 10 more.

The San Juan Consolidated Mining Co. is a combination owning over 15,000 linear feet on South Mountain, comprising a large number of locations of which the Ida is regarded the best. A 30-stamp mill has just been erected and has commenced running. Cropsey's mill was erected by Colonel A. J. Cropsey during the present season (1876) to commence operations in the early part of July 1877. The mill was built for custom work and has four batteries of six stamps each.

C. E. Robins described the Little Annie Mine and the Summit Mining District during the first years of its bonanza in a very informative article published in *The Engineering and Mining Journal* issue of January 26, 1878, on page 57. C. E. Robins was treasurer of The Little Annie Mining Company.

The Little Annie Mine, Summit, Rio Grande County, Colorado
The Highest Gold Mine in the World

The Little Annie, Del Norte, and Margaretta Mines lie near the summit of the Sierra Madre, or main range of the Rocky Mountains, at a mean elevation of about 12,000 feet above the sea. The company's placers, situated in the valley between South Mountain and Summit Peak, and the Little Annie Mill, are about 11,230 feet above tide water. The latter is the highest gold reduction works in the world, as the group of mineral claims on South Mountain are the loftiest gold mines worked or known. Within four miles from the company's office, water flows by the affluents of the Rio Grande into the Gulf of Mexico and by those of the Rio San Juan into the Colorado and Gulf of California.

During the twelve months ending with November 1, 1877, there were at the Summit only 110 days when any outdoor work, saving felling timber, was possible; in other words, 8½ months of the 12 were winter, the ground so heavily snow covered that getting about, save on snow shoes, was impracticable. The average annual temperature, as taken between 7 0'clock A.M. and 9 o'clock P.M., is 32 degrees Fahrenheit. Annual snowfall, 24 feet. The climate does not agree with all persons; both the light air and the continuous cold of the long winters tell upon some constitutions after a prolonged stay. July has been during three years the only month without snowfall. The relation of the foregoing facts to both economical and continuous work are obvious. The present population of the district is 21.

The Annie Mill commenced its first run September 28, 1875, and made during that year 61 days gross time, realizing a product of $28,074.84 in gold, and dividing $3,480.02 among the footholders.

The results of 1875, all things considered, were favorable, and were generally so regarded by those interested.

In the spring of 1876, the snow was eight feet deep on the level, but the work of getting down ore in rawhides and on sleds commenced, and in this manner there was transported down the mountain to the mill dump, between April 23 and May 15, 216 tons, 428 pounds of quartz, which the mill commenced to crush May 20. On May 5, the first party of tramway men reached here by way of the Alamosa in a very heavy snowstorm, which continued until the 8th, when work on the South Mountain Railroad was begun by felling timber for the track. On the 9th, eight carpenters arrived, and the work was pushed steadily forward until its completion on July1. Length, 2125 feet. Work done by contract; bids ranging from $7.50 to $1.50 per foot – built at latter figure in heavy snow, and for the most part in heavy storm; no money made by contractors.

On June 8 the first burro train of the year arrived at the Summit, with goods for the Annie store. On June 16 we cut through the top of the last of the snow tunnels made during the previous winter for communication between the buildings. The first wagons of the year reached the Summit on the 17th. Delivery of ore by tramway during 1876 amounted to 1,469½ tons. Wood bought and used during the twelve months following April 1876, was 1,803 cords; cost, $3,909.39. Net running time of Little Annie Mill in 1876 was 4,777 hours and 56 minutes – 109 days, 1 hour, 56 minutes. Gold production was $63,557.50. The ore house adjoining the Annie Mill, on the south, 42 feet square, capacity 2,500 tons, was begun September 30, and finished October 9. The gulch yielded, in 1876, $518.25 at a cost of $229.12.

In 1877 the mill ran until March 14, when it was shut down for repairs and want of quartz, and the camp was deserted save by parties left in charge of the property. The spring snows were exceptionally heavy (12 feet) as those of the winter had been light, and transportation or outside work of any kind, save snow shoveling, was impossible until June 23. The superintendent and the writer reached here on snow shoes on the evening of May 21. For a month all hands were engaged in shoveling snow from around buildings, and to open road and tramway, both buried up six to nine feet.

F. H. Brandt arrived on June 8 in one of the heaviest and most prolonged snowstorms ever known at the Summit. On the 15th the snow around the company's office was level with the eaves of the building, and the writer walked over the roofs of the adjoining outhouses on snowshoes. The first rain of 1877 was on June 18. The tramway delivered its first carload of ore on June 28, and the Annie Mill recommenced to run on the 25th.

Sluicing in the gulch was commenced on July 2, an average of three hands being employed, and ceased on October 12. July 27 the Pan Mill, erected by Schrontz & Russell, commenced work on Annie and Queen tailings. It was a foolish enterprise, pursued by a foolish method. After a run of eleven days it shut down, having gathered a considerable quantity of ferrous amalgam. Two short runs were subsequently made, with negative results as to profit, and the outfit was abandoned by its owners. The mill is now dismantled, boiler and engine removed from the district, and what little is left, for sale on behalf of creditors.

August 8 brought the first snow of the winter of 1877-8, though no heavy snowstorm occurred until October 11, when 19½ inches fell. In 1877, so far, 1,881 cords of wood, costing

$4,788.63, have been delivered to the company; average, $2.54 per cord; paid in full. The Golden Queen Mill commenced running for the Annie Company under lease at 4:30 P.M., September 15, and stopped for the season at 2:47 A.M., November 5, making between the dates named 1,081 hours 8 minutes net running time, and crushing 382 tons of rock = 8½ tons per 24 hours. Gold product $4,580; cost of same, $1,945.89; yield per ton, $11.99; average yield of Annie Mill during same time, $30.51.

The tramway has so far in 1877 delivered 3,080 tons of ore to the several mills. A 100-foot tunnel into the southern face of the Annie Mine, contracted for at $7.50 per lineal foot, was commenced on October 15, and will be completed within a fortnight.

Mines and Mills

All of the mines were located on a series of northwesterly striking parallel veins. The most southeasterly mines were located east of and not far from the summit of South Mountain. From there the mine workings followed the descending ridge of South Mountain northwesterly to the valley floor where the mills were located. The mines were situated at three locations: the Aztec Mine at the southeastern end of the district; in the middle, the Bobtail Mine; and at the northeastern end, the Little Annie Mine group. (Please refer to the map in the Preface entitled "Plan View of the Gold Ore Zones.")

The first deposits were worked by open cuts or "glory holes," followed by shafts and then tunnels and underground workings. Twelve tunnels were excavated from 1870 to 1885 to develop the various mines.

The Aztec, formerly known as the Summit Mine, was high on the northeastern face of South Mountain. In 1875, ore mined at the surface assayed from $10 to $200 per ton. In 1882 and 1883 the Aztec shipped ore that averaged over $200 per ton and had three shafts and two tunnels. The first discovery of lode gold at Summitville was made by Theodore Goupil at the Aztec Mine, which was originally known as the Esmond Mine. The Aztec group of mines was the earliest development in the district. About 1885 the Iowa Tunnel was driven at a level some 200 feet

Little Annie Mine (P. J. Peterson in front of door)
Photo by J. J. Cornish, Del Norte, circa 1881-1889
Courtesy of the Rio Grande Museum, Del Norte, Colorado

below the Aztec Tunnel. The mine was also worked through the Golconda No. 2 Tunnel.

The Bobtail mine is near the center of the mineralized zone and is separated from the mines on either side by considerable barren ground. The Bobtail was mined through the Bobtail, Highland Mary and Esmond Tunnels.

The Little Annie group of mines were the most productive in the Summitville district and were located on the Annie and Tewkesbury veins which run in a northwest and southeasterly direction not far below the summit of South Mountain. Approximately 5,700 lineal feet of development was done on the Annie vein. The Little Annie Mines were worked through the Winchester, Montroy, French, Ida and Chandler Tunnels. The mines, tunnels, drifts, and mills of the group were located on the Little Annie, Del Norte, Margaretta, Golden Queen, Highland Mary, Chas Brastow, Little Ida and Odin claims, and the Peterson, Brandt and San Juan placers.

Ore haulage from the mines to the mills was first accomplished with wagons during the summer and by sleds and sledges in the winter months. Aerial tramways were then constructed to transport the ore down to the mills from the mines. In 1876, the Little Annie Mining Company constructed a tramway, 2,125 feet long, to carry ore from the Little Annie Mine to its stamp mill in the valley below. The Iowa & Colorado Consolidated Company's tramway, 3,665 feet long and supported by thirty-six trusses, transported ore from the Iowa tunnel portal to the company's mill. It had eighty-four buckets carrying 100 pounds of ore each for a tramway capacity of 150 to 200 tons per day.[2]

Annie and Queen Mills looking up Tramway
Photo Not Dated
Courtesy of the Rio Grande County Museum

After locating the Summit (Aztec) Mine, Dr. Richard F. Adams shipped a small amount of ore to be tested. The test results were positive, and Dr. Adams then located a mill site and ordered a gold processing mill that was erected at Summitville in the fall of 1874. The mill commenced operation in the spring of 1875. In late spring of 1875, machinery for the Little Annie and Golden Queen mills reached Del Norte from Chicago and was hauled to Summitville by mule teams over a road built from Del Norte over Bennett Peak to Summitville that cost $4,000.[3] Thomas Bowen hired Luis Montoya of Del Norte to haul the Little Annie mill machinery from Del Norte to Summitville. Transport of the large pieces required three big ore wagons hooked in tandem and drawn by twenty head of oxen. Montoya was given a generous amount of gold for this successful operation.[4]

The operating mills and their number of stamps in 1881 were: The San Juan Consolidated (Little Ida), thirty; Little Annie, ten; Morey and Sperry, ten; Golden Queen, ten; Iowa & Colorado Consolidated, ten; Missionary, ten; Aztec, five; and Cropsey, twenty-four. The Summitville district had eleven mills with a total of 165 stamps in 1884.

The mills crushed the oxidized ore with stamps, mixed it with water, and passed it over amalgamation plates that were made of copper and coated with mercury or "quick silver." The gold and silver was recovered on the amalgamation plates, and then the gold and silver/mercury amalgamate or alloy was processed on site in a mercury retort. The retort was heated to drive off the mercury as a vapor that was cooled down to its liquid form and re-used on the amalgamation plates. The gold and silver recovered in the retorting process was then melted and cast into bars of dore', a gold/silver alloy.

Historically, the first stamp mill was a heavy boulder to which horizontal poles were tied with strips of hide so that it could be moved up and down by manpower with a drop of several inches to a foot. The next stamps were heavy logs set in guides, lifted by pegs on an extension of the shaft of a water wheel with other pegs near the top of the logs. This process was used in the sixteenth century. The Summitville mills utilized batteries of stamps consisting generally of five heavy cast iron pestles powered by cams on a shaft and rising and falling side by side into a common mortar. The average width of the mortar was about a foot. The length of the mortar was determined by the number of stamps in each battery. Rock was fed into the back of the mortar and water was added, resulting in a pulp of sand-sized or smaller particles.[5]

Because the stamp mills could be sectionalized into weights that could be transported in wagons pulled by oxen, they were ideal for transportation to remote Summitville. Since there was no rail transportation to Del Norte, the Summitville mills had to be transported by wagons over La Veta Pass and across the San Luis Valley to Del Norte. The Rio Grande Railroad commenced work on their Fort Garland division in 1876 and rails were laid to La Veta on the eastern side of La Veta Pass that year. The railroad was extended to Alamosa in the spring of 1878 and then to Del Norte in 1881 to serve the Summitville mines.[6]

Miners and workmen who built the mills and tramways came to Summitville by the hundreds. Charles Ydren rode a stagecoach from Pueblo over La Veta Pass and arrived in Del Norte on October 29, 1873. In 1874 Ydren homesteaded south of the Rio Grande River immediately north of Monte Vista. Swan Anderson came to America in 1866 and also homesteaded land in 1873 near that of Charles Ydren. According the P. J. Peterson's diary he let a contract to Louis Persson and Charles Ydren on May 3, 1876 to build a tramway for $1.50 per foot to be completed on July 8, 1876. On that day, the trial run with ore cars was made, according to P. J. Peterson's diary. Ydren met his future wife, Mary Naslund, at Summitville where she won first place in a beauty contest. They were married May 6, 1884 by a well-known Colorado pioneer – Reverend Alexander Darley.[7]

Placer mining along Wightman Fork continued to about 1880. It is said that considerable placer gold was produced including occasional nuggets.

An article dated August 14, 1880 in Del Norte's *San Juan Prospector* describes the Little Ida Mine:

Bowen's Bonanza – An Interesting Account of a Wonderful Mine

"I tell you, Judge Bowen has a rich mine down there," were the words of a gentleman just returned from the San Juans to a (Denver) Times reporter this morning. *"He has a seventeen foot crevice, and I believe you can't put your finger down without touching free gold."*

Interested by the gentleman's enthusiasm, the reporter asked for further details, which resulted in countless and fabulous rumors that have reached the city lately. Judge Bowen gave as a reason for resigning the lucrative position on the bench recently, that he desired to superintend in person the development of his mine, and there is little doubt but that he acted for his own interest in so doing.

The mine is situated on the continental divide, above timberline, near the border of Rio Grande County, and is twenty-three miles from Del Norte by wagon road. It is 3,300 feet above Del Norte, and the ascent is steep, and arduous. Judge Bowen's mine is situated not far from the Little Annie mine. The crevice is seventeen feet thick, and is a mass of rich gold.

A thirty stamp mill was recently erected, and in the best two days $1,300 were produced. The ore is lying all around the mine in large quantities. Judge Bowen told our informant that he could himself, with a mortar and pestle, stamp out of the heap in one day enough gold to pay off his men for a month. A thief might carry off a small fortune on his back.

The judge (Bowen) is the sole owner of the property, and declares that he would not part with an interest in it to anybody. The rumor that the mine was to be stocked was declared unfounded. He will remain there with his family until the cold weather sets in. Everybody who has visited the mine is convinced that it is the richest one on the continent.

Burchard, in his report for 1881, describes the mining operations in the Summit (Summitville) mining district: the Little Ida Mine owned by the San Juan Consolidated Mining Company is mining a vein reported to contain ten feet in width of decomposed quartz yielding from $1,500 to $2,500 per ton. In about four *months, ore containing $250,000 in gold was mined. The Del Norte adjoins the Little Ida and is a continuation of the same vein. It is owned by the Little Annie Mining Company, which also owns the Little Annie Mine. The Golden Vault is a promising mine owned by the Iowa & Colorado Consolidated Mining Company. The Golconda Company is running a tunnel, now in 200 feet to strike to Golconda lode. Development work was done at the Aztec Mine. Near the foot of the mountain is the Missionary Mine. The ore is refractory and requires roasting before it can be milled. The yield of the principal mines during the portion of the year they were in operation was $289,000. All of the mills in the district are stamp amalgamation mills.[8]*

Buchard, in his report for 1882, states that: *The Little Ida Mine is one of the largest producers. The ore is honeycombed quartz, heavily impregnated with iron oxide and carrying free gold in quantities ranging from $500 to $250,000 per ton. The Little Annie mill will be expanded to fifty stamps in 1883. Owing to an entanglement of affairs of the Golden Queen, the mine was idle during the year. Steady development of the Aztec Mine has provided ore that has paid for the work. This company has shipped all the ore to the smelting works at Pueblo and the mine has paid large dividends. The Golconda group, when developed, will become mines of prominence.[9]*

R. C. Hills[10] was the first to describe gold found in the richest section of the Summitville deposit:

The object of this paper (given at the meeting of March 5, 1883) is a description of the phenomenal ore deposits of Summit District, Rio Grande County, Colorado.

The zone of oxidation extends to a depth varying from a few feet up to 50 fathoms. The quartz is colored dark brown by oxide of iron, and the more highly auriferous material is characterized by an abundance of this oxide. The gold is alloyed with a small portion of silver, about 0.025; otherwise the latter material rarely occurs except with isolated bunches of enargite. All the more valuable bonanzas thus far discovered are confined to this zone. In the Little Ida and Little Annie claims, which are both on the same vein, gold is most abundant near the center of the band, usually in a disseminated form, sometimes as innumerable small grains so aggregated to appear like a thin continuous sheet of metal. Occasionally the grains unite and form flat nuggets, one or more ounces in weight. A large fragment of ore recently taken from the Little Annie contained several such nuggets. The occurrence of this exceedingly rich material is confined to the immediate vicinity of a central channel that has been filled with earth material, fragments of rock and oxide of iron.

In the lower level of the Little Ida, at a depth of 250 feet, aggregations of minute grains and crystals of gold occur in cavities with enargite. In the Aztec Mine is a seam of valuable material from a few inches to a foot or more in width. It is composed of earthy silicates of alumina and magnesia with comminuted vein matter and crystals of barite. The value is about equally divided between the gold and silver. The latter being distributed in specks as a sulfide containing some antimony. The gold is in a very finely divided condition, and is usually of a light snuff color when separated from the rock.

I have already called attention to the connection existing between the gold and hydrous oxide iron in the Summit bonanzas; such connection is by no means rare but in Summit district it is much more intimate than I have heretofore observed. There is no doubt but that pyrite was disseminated originally through the entire mass of quartz and that sulphate of iron, and finally limonite, resulted from oxidation. The latter mineral, rich in gold, is very abundant along the circulating channel near the center of the Little Ida and Little Annie bonanza.

Edwin Eckel[11] describes a Summitville gold specimen and the deposit's mineralogy:

A specimen in the Denver Museum of Natural History from the Aztec mine has dull, dark-colored gold crusts and coatings in a hard limonite matrix. Locally the gold is associated with abundant secondary barite and quartz. Below the oxidized zone are scattered ore bodies of primary ores in resistant pipes and vein-like masses of vuggy quartz with low-grade gold content. They commonly contain pyrite, enargite, some galena and sphalerite, and, at depth substantial amounts of covellite.

A description of the Iowa & Colorado Consolidated Company's property was given in the *San Juan Prospector*[12]: The entrance to the company's mill is through the engine room which contains two boilers and two 50-horsepower engines that furnish power for the mill. Fifty stamps are located on the central floor. In front of the stamps are eight tables, each having two silver plates, and in the rear automatic feeders which supply the stamps with ore from the ore bins. The floor below is fitted up as a silver mill to reclaim silver from the ore. This floor has grinding pans, settlers and jigs that produce concentrate that is sent to the smelter. Along side the grinding pans are clean-up funnels that hold the amalgam as it comes from the silver plates. A retort house is located near the mill. Above the stamp floor is the 300-ton ore bin that receives its ore from the Iowa tunnel by a tramway. The tramway is 3,665 feet long supported by 36 trusses. It has 84 buckets that carry 100 pounds of ore each. The tramway has a capacity of 150 to 200 tons per day. The ore is crushed at the mine by a Blake jaw crusher before being transported by the tramway.

In his 1884 report Burchard states:

The Aztec Mine had shipped ore for over two years that has averaged over $200 per ton. The Iowa & Colorado Mining Company has been idled. The Goldconda Company's tunnel has not yet accomplished its planned ore development. The Little Annie Consolidated Mining & Milling Company plans to run their mine and mill at capacity during the winter. The mine has been cleaned out and placed in shape. The ore is crushed and loaded onto a tramway at the mine and transported to the mill consisting of 12 batteries of 5 stamps each. Here, the ore is finely crushed and washed over the battery plates, which catch a large percentage of the gold, attracted by quicksilver. The tailings are carried to the vanner house where more gold is recovered. The amalgam is retorted and gold bricks cast. The Little Annie is the only operating mill at Summitville.[13]

M. Ed Werner, a mining expert, made the following comments in 1883 about the milling process used by the Summitville mills:[14]

Ever since 1860 I have had considerably to do with ores of the same and similar character, samples of the same being shipped to me in England as an expert to determine their proper treatment, or as a referee, and without having been in the respective mines for examination. I may state this as undoubtedly correct that either Judge Bowen or the other mills will only strike it rich when they hit upon the proper process to extract gold. The mills of Judge Bowen and the Little Annie Co. contained simple stamps with the usual copper plates; however well such machinery is kept, and it was quite a pleasure to look at it, it cannot do much work to advantage. It may treat the surface ore well enough, but as greater depth is reached in the mines it becomes inadequate to the requirements of the ore, which becomes more and more refractory, and more gold runs away with the tailings than is saved on the coppers.

Unfortunately, Werner's 1883 comments proved to be true. Most of the oxidized ore that contained free gold, iron oxides, and quartz had been mined by the end of 1887. Gold recovery from the underlying lower grade sulfide ores was low and did not cover the mining and milling costs. The stamp mills were not adapted to treat the more complex sulfide ores found below the oxidized ore, even though attempts were made by two of the mills to improve recovery. The Little Annie mill installed vanners to recover gold and silver in the amalgamation circuit tailings. A vanner is a short corrugated conveyor belt installed on a slight slope and running uphill. Water introduced near the head of the conveyor washes the lighter material down and off the conveyor. The heavier particles containing the gold and silver remain on the belt and are discharged into a bin at the head of the conveyor. The Iowa & Colorado mill installed a jig circuit to treat the amalgamation tailings and recover silver. Jigs use pulsating water to separate the heavier valuable particles from the lighter barren rock particles.
Even so, production declined. The most productive, the Little Annie Mine, was shut down in 1887, and an exodus from Summitville started and signaled the end of Summitville's bonanza.

Mining Companies

Information about the early day mining companies operating in the Summitville district is taken primarily from Henderson's *Mining in Colorado*[15] and Ellithorpe's *Poker, Politics and Gold*.[16]

During the winter of 1874-75, the owners of the Little Annie mines, Golden Queen, and Golden Star mines entered into contracts with investors for the purpose of developing the mines and installing mills to process the ore. Investors were given an interest in the mines.

The Aztec Company was formed to develop and mine the Aztec Mine, originally owned by R. F. Adams, Lewis Crooke, and LeGrande Dodge. As previously stated, the first mill in the district was erected in 1874 to process Summit mine ores.

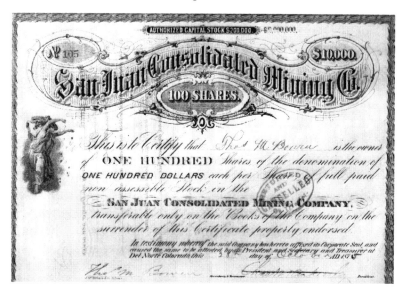

Stock Certificate- San Juan Consolidated Mining Company
Courtesy of Dave Bunk

The San Juan Consolidated Mining Company was incorporated under the laws of the Territory of Colorado on August 25, 1875, with a capital of $2 million consisting of 20,000 shares of stock with a par value of $100 per share. Of the 20,000 shares, 19,000 were issued in the names of owners Charles W. Tankersley, Thomas M. Bowen, Elizabeth J. Gillett, and Charles F. Gillett or George M. Brinkley, who then sold the stock represented by certificates to other individuals. The company's president was Charles W. Tankersley. George M.

Brinkley was vice-president, Thomas M. Bowen was secretary-treasurer, and Charles F. Gilbert was superintendent. Its principal office was in Del Norte, with the right to keep offices in Chicago, New York, and St. Louis. The company owned a large number of claims covering over 15,000 linear feet of vein outcrops on South Mountain. The Little Ida Mine was considered the best. In 1881 the company was operating two stamp mills that processed Little Ida ore — the San Juan Mill and the Odin Mill.

A contract between the San Juan Consolidated Mining Company and George Clay, John A. Taylor, Alva Adams, Morey and Sperry, and Fred Sherwin settled ownership of the Little Ida lode claim. The San Juan Consolidated Mining Company, the owner of the Little Ida applied for a mining patent, and George Clay, et al, were the original claimants of the lode and Little Ida mining claim.[17] The San Juan Consolidated Mining Company did receive a patent on the Little Ida lode claim, Mineral Entry No. 9, on June 14, 1876.[18] The company property was then leased to John Enfield.[19]

P. J. Peterson purchased $2,500 of San Juan Consolidated Mining stock on March 17, 1877 and leased the Queen Mill.[20]

The San Juan Consolidated Mining Company and the Bull Dog Gold Mining Company consolidated on August 28, 1882, and the resulting company was organized and incorporated on September 1, 1882 under the laws of Colorado with Thomas M. Bowen as president and Charles A. Brastow as secretary-treasurer. The Bull Dog Mining Company had previously been incorporated on June 8, 1882 with John Cleghorn, Jr. as president and John E. Hasbrouck and Willard N. Cleghorn directors. The principal office was Del Norte with the right to keep offices in Chicago and New York.

Development of the San Juan Consolidated property would extend to the Bull Dog property; and, since the Bull Dog Mining Company had no milling or tramway facilities, it was determined that the best interests of both companies would be served by consolidation.

A report by Prof. J. Alden Smith, state geologist of Colorado, concerning the company's properties, dated October

15, 1882 and addressed to T. M. Bowen president of the San Juan Consolidated Mining Company, stated:

After thorough examination of the property, I am fully convinced that it is one of the most valuable mining estates present and prospectively, thus far developed in the Rocky Mountains. Profitable as it has been in the past, it needs only energetic and judicious management to be still more profitable in the future.

The property of the San Juan Consolidated Mining Company consisted of the Little Ida and Highland Queen lodes, and the San Juan placer, a tract of land one mile in length and a quarter mile wide. The company also owned the Bowen placer claim, 160 acres situated on the north side of Wightman Fork, where most of the town of Summitville was built. The Bowen was patented by Thomas M. Bowen, John A. McDonald, Charles Brastow, J C. McClennan, Solon W. Pingrey, L. M. Armstrong, John Miles and Maggie T. Bowen on November 11, 1879.[21]

As stated in P. J. Peterson's biography in Chapter 1, Peterson and Brandt sold their shares in the Little Annie Mine in February 1880. The Little Annie Gold Mining Company was incorporated in Colorado on May 20, 1880, with a capital of $5 million, after being sold to New York and Boston investors for $5 million. Johnston Livingston was president and James W. Jessup secretary. The company was originally organized in 1875 as the Little Annie Mining Company. In 1884 the company owned about seventy acres in claims and mill sites and was the only company in the camp running a mill. The company owned the Little Annie, Del Norte and Margaretta Mines.

The Little Annie lode claim, Mineral Survey No. 63; the Del Norte lode claim, Mineral Survey 64; and the Margaretta lode claim, Mineral Survey No. 65 were patented on December 30, 1876, and the patentees were Pear J. Peterson, Ferdinand H. Brandt, Johnston Livingston, John J. Crooke, B. A. Winchester, Eliza S. Winchester, Henry S. Hoyt, Jr., Lewis Crooke and Fran Winchester.[22] Presumably, the patentees were investors in the Little Annie Gold Mining Company.

The Little Annie Gold Mining Company, a New York corporation, was loosely organized and company members were F. H. Brandt, Johnston Livingston, P. J. Peterson, John J. Crook,

Lucius Winchester, LeGrand Dodge, Henry S. Hoyt, Jr., Lewis Clark, and E. S. Winchester. The managers were P. J. Peterson, superintendent, C. E. Robins, treasurer and F. H. Brandt, storekeeper.[23]

Thomas M. Bowen somehow got control of the Little Annie group of mines, which became known as "Bowen's Bonanza," and made his fortune. He managed all of the Little Annie operations. Henry E. Palmer, superintendent of the Little Annie Gold Mining Company, in a report to Thomas M. Bowen, stated that:

In view of the locality in contrasting the mineral bearing mountains of the Rocky Ranges it is not exaggerating to say that Dame Nature was very lavish, seemingly to wasteful profusion, in her wonderful bestowal of such quantity of the matrix of gold. It is safe to say that no other mountain on the continent is to be compared with South Mountain of Summit District in the amount of pure silex. It is a very noticeable fact that nature did her work well in preparing the confines in the wonderful mines of South Mountain.

The first sign of serious problems for the Little Annie Gold Mining Company happened when the stockholders consented to mortgage the property to Marville W. Cooper and Henry S. Hold on November 10, 1883, a debt due November 15, 1888. The mortgage was filed in the State of New York by Johnston Livingston, president, and Thomas Sloan, secretary.[24]

In June of 1887, the Little Annie Gold Mining Company announced it could not meet its payroll and the company shut down mining operations. Miners departed and there was a general exodus from the camp. Summitville was deserted and abandoned. The company's high production bonanza had lasted from 1873 to 1886.

The Iowa & Colorado Consolidated Company owned the Golden Vault Mine as well as other valuable claims in 1882. A mill was built to recover silver and gold, and a tramway was also constructed. In 1884 the company was idle even though it owned nineteen patented mining claims. Its Iowa tunnel had been driven into South Mountain about 1,300 feet. The company's property was sold at a trustee's sale and was bought in trust for the bondholders for $67,838.

An article in the *San Juan Prospector* on November 22, 1884 had this to say:

Stock Certificate – Iowa & Colorado Consolidated Mining Company
Courtesy of Dave Bunk

The greatest drawback to the Iowa Company has been, not the possession of a poor property, but the fact that men in charge of its mining operations were not practical mining men, and the natural result, ill-directed efforts, has almost discouraged stockholders.

This company has the finest buildings, tramway and machinery in the Summit. The Iowa company experience has demonstrated the fact that a man may be a good merchant, banker, lawyer or governor, but that he cannot conduct mining operation without the cooperation of practical miners.

The Iowa & Colorado property was sold at a trustee's sale last Wednesday and was bought by A. E. Martin in trust for the stockholders.

Stock Certificate – The Golconda Gold Mining Company
Courtesy of Dave Bunk

The Golconda Gold Mining Company was incorporated January 1, 1880 with a capital of $2 million represented by 200,000 shares having a par value of $10 each share. Thomas Bowen owned 125,400 shares and was president, Charles W. Taylor, secretary, and Columbus W. Burris, director. The company's principal office and place of business was Del Norte, with the right to keep offices in Leadville, Colorado, Chicago and New York. Thomas M. Bowen also served as superintendent and general manager and received an annual salary of $3,600 payable monthly for his services. In 1881 the company excavated or drove a tunnel, called a drift in mining terminology, to the Golconda lode. By 1882 the company had six claims, and in 1883 it produced eighty tons of ore averaging $50 per ton. The tunnel had not developed the ore the company had planned for in 1884, leaving the company with an indebtedness of $106,000.

The Golden Queen Mine organizers were Johnston Livingston, John J. Crook, Arthur Burton, O. P. Posey, Alva Adams — who later became the governor of Colorado three times, J. S. Reef, and others. J. S. Reef was superintendent and J. L. Beamer was the bookkeeper.[25] O. P. Posey and Alva Adams sold 45 2/3 feet of the Golden Queen lode to William Van Gieson for $4,666 on December 11, 1875.[26]

Other less important mining companies were organized during Summitville's bonanza period. They included the Golden Star Gold & Silver Mining Company, the Odin Gold Mining Company, the Bowen Bonanza Mining Company, the Little Jessie Segregated Mining Company and the Missionary Mine. There were, no doubt, others.

Thomas M. Bowen was a corporate officer for the Odin Gold Mining Company, the Bowen Bonanza Mining Company, and the Little Jessie Segregated Mining Company as well as the San Juan Consolidated Mining Company.

Thomas M. Bowen

Thomas Meade Bowen was indeed the 'Midas" of Summitville and one of Colorado's prominent mining investors. He was born on October 26, 1835 in Burlington, Iowa, was educated at Mount Pleasant, Iowa, and began practicing law at the age of eighteen.[27] He served one term in the Iowa House of Representatives before moving to Kansas. He fought with the Union Army during the Civil War where he advanced to the rank of brigadier general in 1863. After the war he settled in Little Rock, Arkansas, where he married Margarette Thurston. He established himself as a lawyer and was involved in the turbulent politics during the period of Reconstruction after the Civil War. He served as a member of the Arkansas Supreme Court for four years until he was appointed to be governor of the Territory of Idaho in 1871 for a short tenure by President Grant. He returned to Arkansas the same year. He ran but lost a bid to become a U. S. Senator from Arkansas. Bowen then moved his family to Del Norte, Colorado in January 1875, where he started a successful law practice.

Shortly after arriving in Del Norte, he became involved in mining ventures in the San Juan Mountains, particularly at Summitville. His first trip to Summitville was in July 1875, when there were snowdrifts eleven feet deep across the road. He invested in mines and prospects and provided grubstakes to prospectors.

T. M. Bowen's Little Ida Tunnel (Bowen leaning against tree)
Photo by J. J. Cornish, Del Norte, circa 1881-1889
Courtesy of the Rio Grande County Museum, Del Norte, Colorado

He first gained control of and then acquired the mining claims that were later called "Bowen's Bonanza."[28]

He was elected Judge of the Fourth Judicial District on November 1, 1876, serving until May 25, 1880, when he resigned in order to devote full time to his mining ventures. As judge he supposedly held court in the tunnel of the Little Ida Mine where he was superintendent for the Little Annie group of mines on South Mountain.[29]

The *Ouray Times*, in an article dated April 1, 1882, said:

Judge Bowen arrived in Lake City to hold the first term of court. At that time the judge was not blessed with a superabundance of worldly goods; his clothes were decidedly the worse for wear, but he stood up under the frown of fortune wonderfully and was a "hail fellow well met" with the boys.

The *San Juan Prospector* published an obituary of Thomas Bowen in its January 5, 1907 issue that, in part, said:

He entered upon the practice of law at Del Norte and soon after was elected judge of the fourth judicial district which at that time included almost the entire southwestern quarter of the state.

He held court at Del Norte, Saguache, Lake City, Fairplay and other points. The members of the bar in those days moved around very much the same as the court, and some of the stories that are told have to do with the blending of judicial decorum and an entirely different attitude toward life when night came and the crime was laid aside.

Many stories are told of threats against the life of the judge and of the promptness with which Judge Bowen, who then personified "law across the range," met such threats and continued to visit justice against offenders unawed by promises of personal violence.

Bowen was elected to the Colorado House of Representatives in 1882 and a year later was elected to the U. S. Senate from Colorado. He served one term of six years in the Senate and chaired the Committee on Mines and Mining. He was a champion of free coinage of silver, federal irrigation projects in the West, and federal aid for public schools.[30] He then returned to Colorado and continued his involvement in mining ventures.

An interesting story about Bowen having problems traveling to Denver from Summitville was published in the *Denver Inter-Ocean Press* in 1882. The story, in the form of a ballad entitled *Tom Bowen's Ride*, tells of Bowen leaving Summitville one fall day to attend the Convention of the Colorado General Assembly in Denver and hurrying down the twenty miles to Del Norte. He missed his train by three minutes and hired some men to follow the train to Alamosa by handcar that he helped pump. Unfortunately they arrived in Alamosa too late to catch the Denver train. He then paid a railroad engineer to commandeer an engine and catch up to the train on the east side of La Veta Pass. Bowen was the fireman shoveling coal into the steam engine's

Annie's Store and Post Office, Undated
Courtesy of the Rio Grande County Museum

firebox during the chase. The trip was a success, as Bowen ascended to the U. S. Senate within three months.[31]

Bowen built a mansion in Pueblo, Colorado, now listed in the National Register of Historic Places. He died in Pueblo on December 30, 1906.

Summitville Town Site

The town of Summitville was never incorporated and originally was comprised of three camps – Iowa, Sunnyside, and Summitville. The town was named for Dr. Adam's Summit Mine. Summitville was a company town, built on mining company property, and remained so throughout its history.

Summitville was first occupied all winter in 1875, which was a relatively mild winter, by miners who built cabins. The first post office, known as Summit, was established February 10, 1876 and discontinued September 24, 1879. It re-opened October 1879, and the post office name was changed to Summitville on November 17, 1880.[32]

In his report for 1875, Raymond describes Summitville's town site and living conditions.[33]

The population of the district is about 200. Del Norte, 27 miles distant to which access is had by a wagon road built this year and by a trail down Piños Creek, is its supply point. Besides the mills and their outbuildings, there are about 50 cabins in the settlement, built of logs and covered with dirt. Freight from Del Norte varies from 1½ to 10 cents per pound. Wood is the only fuel. Cost of lumber $30 per thousand board feet; potatoes 1 to 8 cents per pound; flour, $8.75 per hundred; tea, $1.25 to $1.50 per pound; beef, 7½ cents per pound; bacon, 22½ cents per pound; sugar, 18 to 20 cents per pound; onions, 12½ cents per pound; dried apples, dried peaches and dried currants, 20 cents per pound; kerosene, $1 per gallon. All supplies must be laid in before winter opens. No raising of vegetables has yet been attempted, though it is possible that a very few of the hardier kinds might succeed.

One of the first ski clubs in Colorado, if not the first, was organized at Summitville. The March 13, 1877 issue of the San Juan Prospector carried the following tongue-in-cheek story about the club written by its vice president, Jacob Reef, entitled "Summit Snow-Shoe Club:"

The institution was organized on the 18th of February by the election of E. C. Goodrich as president and C. E. Robins, secretary. It may, perhaps, be considered a sort of adjunct to the Zenith Lyceum. The shoes used are the Norwegian – some ten feet long, made of pine, and inaugurated the proceedings of the club by a snow-shoe race, a brief account of which may interest some of your readers.

Beyond question this is the most unconscionable ludicrous performance ever devised by the wit of man, when essayed by a non-expert, as most of the contestants were. When a man gets to going down a mountain side at a mile a minute and begins to lose his balance, and after indescribable flexations of all sorts, ends by describing a bodily trajectory over the snow much as he would do if shot out of an Armstrong gun – one shoe a hundred feet in advance, and the other, trying to catch up, a hundred feet behind – there is nothing to do but laugh. Such is especially the case when a grave and ever-minded person, like Prof. Robins, leaving for the once those profound problems of geology, which he spreads before us at the Lyceum, gives us a free exhibition of his agility in turning summersaults – more especially still where the performer is a large, stately-looking man like P. J. Peterson, when 200 pounds go ricocheting over the boundless feather-bed which at this season covers the slopes of the Sierra Madre – head, arms, legs and trunk in a state of such confusion that it would drive the best anatomist on earth into a craze to attempt an identification of the several members. The Laplander is the star snowman of the district. He is our expert, and, bracing himself, he starts on the mile race. Slowly at first, then like a petrel over a glassy sea, we watch his descent from below. It becomes a flight, the highest poetry of terrestrial motion. I have seen men make faster time today on two sticks of pine lumber that is recorded of any railroad. He goes now like a rifle ball, but some slight obstacle begets confusion in his perfect poise, and he begins to sway and waver; no stopping or slacking to "recover." Outward lies his way. The bud of a mountain willow, a quid of tobacco on the spotless snow, a pennyweight too much ballast on either side of the median line, and he goes head or feet foremost under the stern doctrine of the resolution of forces, into that mighty featherbed stern foremost, generally. The Laplander, however, is not down yet; perhaps he will retrieve – he is good at that. The Summit atmosphere is still as a sleeping child, but his quick progress makes the wind whistle arcticly and articulately about him. We watch his swift progress with sincere and hearty admiration. But one shoe strikes that quid; he feels it instantly, and the quick and subtle electromotive centers for readjustment. We scoffers, waiting for our fun – see from afar the stiffening of the back, and we know that "Lap's" tarsal muscles are under heavy strain. He begins to bend and bow like our grand forests in a western gale. We watch breathlessly – he may regain the center of gravity, but no. He slides, falters, falls. Down he goes, and onward. He will burrow thirty feet in Summit feathers before he "gets up and dusts." Silently we await his emergence. When he is within speaking distance, he burrows out. We suspend our mirth until he digs himself into the light of day, and await his cheerful utterance. It comes – after a pat of snow has been ejected from his mouth, and his lungs have taken in enough air for speech – "For God's sake – hell!"

The "School of the Snow-shoe" takes in daily at one o'clock P.M. when all members are expected to be on hand to go through "drill." Philosophical questions pertaining to the laws of accelerated motion are to be discussed twice a week. The question selected for the first debate was this: "Phillip Kuhn's place where he sits down is thirteen inches in traverse diameter, by accurate measurement taken at the signal office." Yesterday at the end of the disastrous run down a 45-degree grade, he "sat down." The imprint of this action was a circular depression three feet deep and five feet four inches in diameter. Required – the rationale between the die and the depression, and the full explanation thereof, which mathematical formulae illustrate the entire transaction. Full details to be reported for the* San Juan Prospector. *Several learned papers are already in process on this question. Who wouldn't be a Summiter?*

The first paragraph of the preceding newspaper article states that the Summit Snow-Shoe Club is an adjunct to the Zenith Lyceum. According to P. J. Peterson's diary of 1877 the Zenith Lyceum was a literary society active at Summitville.[34] Rather unusual for a mining camp in the wilderness.

M. Ed Werner described the town of Summitville and life therein in an article published in 1883:[35]

Summitville consists so far of one hotel, the Bowen House, a score or so of saloons, one livery stable, six or seven boarding houses, and a few stores, besides three stamp mills. I would advise anyone desirous of taking produce or anything else there to make arrangements before hand how to dispose of his stuff. Without this it is very risky to take either hay, potatoes, grain, or anything else. It might not be possible to find a purchaser, the place is too small as yet to offer a market. As for people coming out here to find work there are the mills which pay good wages – about $40 to $50 a month and board – but employ only a limited number of hands, and as Judge Bowen told me and as I saw for myself overflowed with men; then there is a little building and fixing up in town and chopping cord-wood and hauling of the same. The price of either is from $1.50 to $2 per cord, according *to distance from town, etc., a price which leaves very poor wages taking in consideration the cost of living and the naturally high charges for stabling of horses, hay, oats, etc. In consequence of the high altitude – near timberline – very little camping out and that sort of thing can be done if at all, so at almost all times all outdoor work has to be done in the snow or else in the sludge resulting from the melting of the same. There is, of course, plenty of room for prospectors. Their best time will probably be from the beginning of August til the setting in of winter snowstorms. What chances there may be for them to find new leads and how to make them valuable by sale or otherwise, quien sabe. I should not advise anyone to go except he can take a little money with him.*

Summitville was connected to Del Norte by telephone in 1883.[36] By 1886 the population of Summitville had grown to 600, mail was delivered three times a week, a newspaper, the Summitville Nugget, *printed the news, and there were fourteen saloons in town.*[37]

The *San Juan Prospector* in its November 22, 1884 issue described activities in Summitville:

The mercantile portion of Summitville at present is conducted principally by Jesse J. Crosswy, general merchandise; Chapman & Weiss, drugs and notions; and John Ewing, Jr., hardware. Winter has set in and many of the business houses that were in operation during the summer have been closed down until spring. The ladies of Summitville are doing a good work in keeping up a Sunday school. An entertainment and Christmas tree will be indulged in during the holidays.

Transportation to and from Summitville was difficult at best and almost impossible during the winter months except by skis or snowshoes. The first road from Del Norte followed the West Fork of Frisco Creek over Bennett Mountain and was used by the miners to haul machinery and by Alden Bassett's wagons to transport freight to the camp. A road along Piños Creek from Del Norte was completed in 1875. In 1888 it became a much improved toll road and was extended over South Mountain to Platoro by way of Stunner on the Alamosa River. It joined the military road built from Fort Garland in the San Luis Valley to Fort Lewis at Pagosa Springs on the west side of the Continental

Divide. Barlow and Sanderson stagecoaches were traveling from the Denver and Rio Grande Railroad terminal at Del Norte to Summitville in 1881.[38]

The U. S. Congress authorized construction of the military road and appropriated $5,000 for the work in 1878. The road ran due west from Alamosa across the San Luis Valley to Rio los Gatos (Cat Creek) and then over a low divide to the Alamosa River. It followed the Alamosa River to its ascent of 1,550 feet to the Continental Divide (Elwood Pass) in five miles. The grading from the summit west was not completed in 1878. Construction of approximately twenty-three miles of road down the East Fork of the San Juan River remained to complete the road.[39]

Walter Comly wrote letters to his mother and father describing his trips to and from Summitville. In a letter from the Ruder Hotel, written on September 5, 1882, he describes the trip from Del Norte to Summitville as follows:[40]

Left Del Norte at 9:30 AM for a twenty-eight mile ride in the stage, and to see better, rode outside with the stage driver. I only wish you could take that ride, for a ways anyhow, but am afraid you would feel uncomfortable before you got here. The fore part of the drive was delightful until we got up to an elevation of about 11,000 feet, and then it began to make me feel a little uncomfortable. After a little it grew very cold, and when we got to about 12,000 feet up it began to snow, so I put on my coat. The storm ceased after a while but I continued to feel more uncomfortable, till when we reached the summit of the range, 13,500 feet above tide water, 8,000 [sic. 6,000] feet higher than Del Norte, and that a terrible rise in such a short ride. I felt so dizzy I could hardly see. I felt a buzzing in my ears and felt as if I could not get my breath, and my heart seemed to work like a steam engine, and then my nose commenced to bleed, and after that stopped I felt better and continued to feel more and more comfortable as we came down from the summit to Summitville, which is four miles from the summit and at an elevation of 11,500 feet. I had a bad headache all night, and a little nose bleed this morning, but feel first rate now.

In a letter to his father written October 16, 1882 at the Windsor Hotel in Del Norte, Comly described his trip to Del Norte as follows:[41]

Well, here I am in Del Norte on my way to Denver, leaving the wilds of Colorado perhaps forever, and a fine time I have had in them too. We (Elwood and I) left our cabin early seventh day morning, packed all my things on our backs and started for our long hard walk of a little over ten miles. We got to the Summit a little after noon. It took us about five hours to make the trip. We were pretty tired and my feet were almost frozen walking through the deep snow, but still I got along better than I had feared. But my wind is so good now it did not blow me much more than Uncle Elwood. Found out when we got to the Summit the stage did not run on Sunday on account of the cold and snow, so had to lay over there until today. Almost all who can have left the Summit and our stage was full today. We brought down a man affected by the altitude, and a large wagon brought down a sick woman with the same trouble. What does thee think they charge a ton for freighting to the Summit when the snow gets deep, $200 a ton for seven miles. We met several teams on the road with twelve oxen, and thirteen or fourteen mules, and then they can only haul a ton at a load and it takes four or five days for the trip. (Note: Elwood Pass was named after Comly's Uncle Elwood).

A Stagecoach Holdup

The final incident of Summitville's bonanza was the attempted robbery of the last gold shipment from the Little Annie Mill. The Little Annie Gold Mining Company shut down operations in June of 1887. The ore that was on hand at the shutdown was milled and a final "cleanup" of gold occurred the following August. The resulting gold brick was being transported from Summitville to Del Norte by stagecoach for shipment to the mint when the attempted robbery happened. It is best described in an article that appeared in Monte Vista's San Luis Graphic, August 26, 1887.

DARING HIGHWAY ROBBERY
Supt. Watson and Assistant Supt. Burton Held Up By Two Robbers with Rifles!
Ten Thousand Dollar Gold Brick The Prize Fought For
A Miraculous Escape With The Gold!

Del Norte, August 24, 1887. (Special to the *San Luis Valley Graphic*)

Del Norte was thrown into a fever of excitement Tuesday by a telephone message from Osgood's mill, 16 miles above town, on the Summit road calling for a doctor to attend Superintendent Watson of the Annie Mine, who had been shot by some "hold-ups," and that Asst. Sup't. Burton had been shot also, but not found.

Immediately the Sheriff had a posse of thirteen mounted, and within an hour from the receipt of the news they were off. The Sheriff with nine of his posse started for the scene of the trouble, while four others under the leadership of L. B. Shaw, took the trail up Francisco Creek, toward Del Norte Mountain and Cornwall.

Later news from Osgood's was to the effect that Burton had arrived there with the bullion safe, and only slightly wounded in the hand and that Sup't. Watson was not dangerously shot.

About 7 o'clock in the morning Sup't. Watson with Ass't Burton left Summitville with a brick of gold from the "last cleanup" weighing about 75 pounds. When about an eighth of a mile this side of the old toll-gate, they were fired upon from the brush, not more than a rod from the carriage without warning. Burton threw himself from the wagon, instantly, and fell by the side of the road, where he played dead, for a minute or two. The horses leaped forward at a furious rate. Watson holding the lines trying to manage them, but the horses were unmanageable and a few rods further on the wagon was overturned, throwing Mr. Watson to the ground and burying him under the robes and contents of the carriage. Burton, finding the coast clear got to where the wagon upset, found the valise containing the gold, grabbed it and jumped for the brush, and with his wits about him, took to the thickets and rocky places, hiding and skulking for four hours or more, arriving at Osgood's about 1 P.M., with the 75 pound brick, and nearly exhausted.

Mr. Lempke, the driver of the Summitville mail stage, was a quarter of a mile ahead of Watson and Burton when the affair occurred. He heard no firing but was apprised of something having happened to the team behind, by being overtaken by one of the horses of Watson's team tearing along the road with its harness on. He immediately stopped the runaway horse, and thinking some accident had happened, turned about to render them assistance. After going a short distance the other horse was seen coming down the road with part of the neck yoke and some parts of the harness, disarranged. A few rods further on he met Mr. Watson on the run, following the horses, bare headed, and apparently dazed and unable to give any account of what had occurred. Seeing blood on his coat, Mr. Lempke surmised that Mr. Watson was a little off, and that something serious had happened. After considerable persuasion Mr. Watson was induced to get on the mail stage and was driven to Osgood's, where he was soon able to give a clue to what had occurred.

An immediate search was made for Burton, but no trace of him could be discovered, showing how carefully he had covered his tracks.

While still searching for Burton, the sheriff's posse arrived from Del Norte, and instead of immediately following the trail the robbers had made, Mr. Lempke says an hour or more was lost when time was most valuable, as the robbers being ahead, made deep tracks in their flight, and it being late in the afternoon, and heavy shower clouds overhanging and threatening every hour of daylight was precious.

Mr. Lempke believes that a prompt and vigorous pursuit would have overtaken the robbers or located them, so they could easily have been corralled, but darkness soon covered the trail, and the pursuers were compelled to return to Osgood's for the night.

The trail of the robbers, as far as followed, showed their course to be towards the Conejos camp at Jasper, but up to the present time everything regarding their whereabouts is merely conjecture.

P. S. – Watson has just been brought in to Del Norte. He has a flesh wound in the left side just under the arm, which is not serious. He suffers more from the concussion than the wound.

Additional Particulars

The sheriff's posse has been scouring the mountains in every direction. The trail of the robbers has been followed to the head of Piños Creek. The trail shows that two men did the deed. One has heavy boots and broad soles, the other with lighter boots *and high heels. One of which was considerably turned over on the side as he walked. Marshall Cullumber and Constable Hoyt on orders from Sheriff Cleghorn, scoured the country in the region of Jasper and the Conejos mining camp. Marshall White and Deputy Sheriff Brodie of Del Norte have been at the head of Rock Creek without results. The highwaymen were masked.*

Later it was found that two men, Harris and O'Connel, were the highwaymen. Harris was arrested and thrown into the Del Norte jail. O'Connel, a onetime Summitville miner, was arrested in Saguache. O'Connel and his wife had lived in Del Norte for a time before going to work at Summitville. O'Connel's wife planned the holdup and made the masks. Nothing is known about O'Connel after his arrest or in later life; but Harris, in jail awaiting trial, with the help of John McCann and another man bound, gagged and shot Jean Renner, Deputy Sheriff and John Hocker, Sheriff, and escaped jail. A posse was formed and a hunt for the escapees commenced. Juan Valdez, who was hauling wood from the Twin Mountain area, reported a campfire he had seen on the north side of the mountains. An individual taking supplies to a sheep camp nearby was intercepted. Since the McCann family lived nearby, the posse suspected that these supplies were from them. O'Connel, McCann and the third man's camp was located and the posse of six men surrounded it at break of day. With careful aim they killed the three men as they slept.[42]

The end of bonanza times at Summitville was confirmed in an article in the January 14, 1888 issue of the San Juan Prospector:

The Little Annie work at Summitville was discontinued this week and the hands paid off in accordance with the advice of the company's attorneys. The indicators now are that the San Juan and Annie companies will do nothing at all next season, unless through a compromise or sale, which is hardly possible.

CHAPTER 3
SLOW TIMES
1888-1926

Main Street of Summitville, circa 1890
Courtesy of the Monte Vista Historical Society

Mining of gold and silver was greatly reduced during Summitville's slow years primarily because of 1) metallurgy to economically treat the ore from the lower grade sulfide ores was not available, 2) the repeal of the Sherman Silver Purchase Act of 1890 and, 3) the panic of 1907. Most of Summitville's mining companies went out of business after the bonanza and their properties were sold. Two outside investors – Albert Eugene Reynolds and Theodore N. Barnsdall ultimately purchased most of the properties and planned to consolidate their holdings into one corporation. This did not occur until after the deaths of both. Production from 1888 through 1925, thirty-seven years, amounted to 21,500 troy ounces of gold and 70,000 troy ounces of silver compared to 94,000 troy ounces of gold and 107,000 troy ounces of silver during the bonanza period of twelve years. Copper and lead were first recovered from the sulfide ores in 1896. The greatest copper production during the period occurred in 1901 (65,600 pounds) and in 1912 (29,700 pounds). There was no production at Summitville in 1907, 1909, 1916, and 1918 through 1922.

In 1889 Summitville's population was twenty-five including three "ladies of the evening." The town was deserted in 1893.[1]

No gold and only 800 troy ounces of silver were produced at Summitville in 1893, the year of the repeal of the Sherman Silver Purchase Act of 1890 that required the government to purchase millions of ounces of silver with paper currency that could be redeemed for silver or gold. Congressmen from the western silver states had sufficient power in 1890 to force its passage through Congress. The price of silver climbed to $1.50 per troy ounce from $0.84, almost doubling its price overnight. This price assured increased silver production from the western states, particularly from Colorado's San Juans.

However, it was felt by some that the act was in part responsible for the "Panic of 1893," as it helped create a lack of confidence in the government's fiscal policies. Investors turned the paper notes in for gold dollars, thus depleting the government's gold reserve that backed the country's currency. People were out of work and banks were closed. Congress was called into a special session on August 7, 1893 by President Cleveland to repeal the Sherman Silver Purchase Act, but the Senate delayed the repeal until October 1893. The price of silver dropped from $0.83 to $0.62 per troy ounce in four days after the repeal. This essentially stopped the mining of silver in the West and severely impacted mining at Summitville, even though gold was that area's primary metal.

Most Summitville mining companies went out of business after the district's bonanza. On February 12, 1890, the Little Jesse Segregated Mining Company was sold to Thomas M. Bowen for $1,000 owed to him for advances the company was unable to pay back. The entire property of the company consisted of the south 700 feet of the Little Jesse lode and the Omega and Omega No. 2 claims, together with all machinery, tools, implements, engines, boilers, boiler parts of stamp mill and all other machinery owned.[2] In addition, many mining claims were sold by Rio Grande County for delinquent taxes.

However, two of the more successful companies were sold to outside investors, Albert Eugene Reynolds and Theodore N. Barnsdall. Barnsdall, a prominent oilman from Pittsburgh, met A. E. Reynolds for the first time on a train as both men were traveling to New York City. On learning that Reynolds was a Colorado mine operator, Barnsdall proposed to join him in mining ventures and did so.

Albert Eugene Reynolds

Albert Eugene Reynolds was born on February 13, 1840, in Niagara County, New York, one of ten children. Reynolds attended Madison University, later named Colgate University. At the close of the Civil War, he left home for Kansas with $80 in his pocket and worked for a mercantile firm near Leavenworth. He then joined his brother in establishing a store in Richmond, Missouri, and shortly thereafter went further west to Fort Lyon, Colorado, where he was the "sutler," or trader, who sold goods to the soldiers at the post store.

In 1869, Reynolds and W. M. D. Lee formed a partnership to sell merchandise to the Arapaho and Cheyenne tribes. The business was very successful while the Indians had buffalo hides to trade for goods. When their Indian trade fell off after the slaughter of the buffalo herds, the partners sold merchandise to the military and cattlemen from stores at Fort Supply, 100 miles south of Dodge City, Kansas, and Fort Elliott in the Texas Panhandle. They branched out into freighting and ranching. The partnership was terminated in 1882.

Reynolds married Dora Earll in Columbus, Wisconsin, on April 25, 1883. They lived in Lake City, Colorado a short time and then relocated to Denver after their only child, Anna Earll Reynolds, was born. The Reynolds were long-time residents of Denver. He continued merchandising and freighting for several years until he turned his efforts toward mining ventures for the first time. He first involved himself in mining operations at Lake City, Colorado. Evidently Reynolds didn't find any mining properties at Lake City that suited him, but the experience started him on a lifetime of acquiring mining properties in most of the western states.

He then directed his attention to the mining districts near Ouray, Colorado. There, like Tom Walsh, he struck it rich. He and Hubbell Reed developed the Virginius Mine by driving the Revenue Tunnel, started in 1883 and completed in 1893, into the ore body at a depth of 3,000 feet below its outcrop. The ore was dropped to the tunnel level by gravity for haulage out of the mine instead of being hoisted to the surface through a shaft. This method dramatically reduced the cost of mining, provided good ventilation and easy access to the workings, and eliminated the cost of pumping water to the surface through a shaft. The Virginius Mine was the first all-electric powered mining operation in Colorado. Mules that hauled ore through the Revenue Tunnel were replaced by electric locomotives in 1896.

Reynolds' revolutionary approach to low-cost mining convinced mining investors, particularly from the East, to fund his projects throughout the mining districts of Colorado. He maintained control of his mining companies by holding a majority of the stock.

The repeal of the Sherman Silver Purchase Act in 1893 started a precipitous decline in the value of Reynolds' mining properties. A millionaire at age fifty, he was approaching insolvency when he died. Even though he was still worth $2 million on paper, his mine holdings could not be liquidated. Reynolds passed away at his daughter's home in Hickory, Tennessee, on March 21, 1921.

A. E. Reynolds' only child, Anna Reynolds Morse, inherited her father's mining properties. Anna married Bradish P. Morse, a member of the Morse Brothers Machinery Company. After Reynolds' death Morse looked after his wife's properties.

Theodore N. Barnsdall

Theodore Newton Barnsdall was born in Titusville, Pennsylvania on June 10, 1851, to William and Fidelia Barnsdall. William was responsible for beginning the Barnsdall oil legacy. He drilled the second commercial oil well in American history and built the first oil refinery in Titusville during the winter of 1860-61.

After a brief period spent at a preparatory school in New York, Theodore Barnsdall returned to Pennsylvania and began working for the Barnsdall Oil Company as a pumper on one of his father's wells. At the age of sixteen he drilled his first oil well near Titusville. He then drilled a number of successful wells in Pennsylvania's Bradford Field and built a foundation for his later mid-continent operations.

When the Indian Territory Illuminating Oil Company's Osage lease was broken, Theodore Barnsdall acquired 334,000 acres of leases in the oil-rich Osage land. After succeeding his father as president of the Barnsdall Oil Company, he was able to build it into a major energy operation. The company had extensive holdings in Oklahoma. The community of Barnsdall (formerly Bigheart, named for James Bigheart, chief of the Osage Indian tribe), Oklahoma, site of substantial company operations, carried his name. In terms of drilling wells and opening new territory, Barnsdall was one of the most aggressive entrepreneurs and oil operators in the history of the business and was the largest independent oil producer of his times in the United States. He also served as president or board chairman of the Kansas Natural Gas Company, the Pittsburgh Oil and Gas Company, and the Union Natural Gas Corporation. In 1905, he was a partner in founding the Alaska-Pacific Railroad and Terminal Company, formed to develop the anthracite coal deposits in Alaska.

On June 22, 1881, Theodore Barnsdall married Louisa Angela Stitt. They had a daughter, Aline. His relationship with his wife was a stormy one. He tried to divorce her and when she refused, he proceeded to have a second child by another woman. Aline built a residence, the Hollyhock House in Los Angeles, California about 1927. The house was nominated for a national historic landmark.

The *New York Times* issue of February 18, 1917, carried Theodore N. Barnsdall's obituary:

Pittsburgh, February 27 - *Theodore N. Barnsdall, president of the Pittsburgh Oil and Gas Company and the Union Natural Gas Corporation, and for many years one of the most widely known oil and mining operators in the United States died at his home today in his sixty-seventh year. He was born in Titusville, Pennsylvania, and began life as a poor young man in the oil fields. He was said to be worth more than $15 million. Mr. Barnsdall was the founder of the Kansas Natural Gas Company, and as a member of the Barnsdall Oil Company he held large oil properties in Oklahoma, California, and other southwestern states.*

Mining Companies

A. E. Reynolds purchased the Golconda Mining Company in June 1891 and then sold three-eighths of it to Charles P. Palmer, through whom he had acquired the company whose claims covered nearly one-half of the mining district.[3] Thomas Bowen tendered his resignation as president and director of the company on July 2, 1891. A. E. Reynolds was then elected president of the company on August 1, 1891 at a meeting in Denver.[4]

Reynolds anticipated that he could dispose of a substantial block of the enterprise's stock to his friends in the East. This proved impossible because Palmer, as superintendent, could not find high-grade shipping ores. What he found was low-grade ore, which Reynolds conceded was of little use to anybody and could not be treated with available technology to produce a concentrate that could be shipped to a smelter profitably.[5]

The Reynolds Tunnel, originally the Golconda Tunnel, was driven into the Tewksbury vein in 1897 but was abandoned in 1906. It is the longest, lowest tunnel at Summitville. The Reynolds Tunnel was an attempt to develop the mine at a low level to provide ventilation and drainage for the workings, and the cheapest method of ore transportation to the surface as was done at the Virginius Mine and Creede's Commodore Mine.

An article in the *Monte Vista Journal* of January 19, 1901 told about the Golconda (Reynolds) Tunnel:

<u>About Summitville</u> – *Steady progress has been made on the Golconda tunnel at Summitville during the past year, under the management of Charles F. Palmer, and the future looks very hopeful. About 2,000 feet is the distance penetrated in 1900, including the drift. The men are now drifting to the north towards the Annie workings. About 700 feet remains before the objective point is reached, which manager Palmer expects to occur by May next. The ground now being worked is very bad and has to be timbered to within two feet of the breast. The chief difficulty is the want of good air, and to remedy this a ventilating line is now being put in, consisting of boxing 10 x 10 inches for a length of 1820 feet, although a mile of work as been accomplished altogether without ventilation. The new ventilation work is expected to reach the breast by January 20th. Several copper veins have been crossed, but no development has been attempted, nor will there be any until the Annie workings are reached and fresh air is obtained. In Mr. Palmer's opinion, copper will be the great thing at Summitville in the future and gold merely a by-product.*

The *Monte Vista Journal* issue of September 1, 1900 describes an accident in the Reynolds Tunnel:

An accident occurred in the big tunnel at Summitville last Saturday night by which two miners came near losing their lives. Frank Clark and John Scarff were working in the breast of the tunnel taking out an unexploded piece of powder when an explosion occurred frightfully mangling both of them. It was thought for a time that Frank Clark could not survive and would in any event lose both eyes and Scarff was badly injured about the face and breast. Dr. McFadzean of Del Norte was sent for to dress the wounds, and the sufferers were brought to Del Norte where by good care and close attention it is thought that Clark, who was found to be most seriously hurt, will recover the sight of one eye and other than slight scars will come out all right. Superintendent Palmer did all in his power to alleviate the suffering and no blame is attached to anyone, as it was one of those unfortunate things that occur so often in the mines.

On June 14, 1892, the court ordered, adjudged and decreed all the mortgaged property of the Little Annie Gold Mining Company be sold at public auction by the sheriff, in one parcel and as an entirety, and on July 28, 1892, the Little Annie, Del Norte and Margaretta mining claims and the Livingston, Winchester, Queen, Peterson, Brandt, Cooper, Jessup and Hoyt placers claims owned by the company, and all personal property of every kind or nature around the premises of the company, including the tools and machinery were sold by John Cleghorn, Sheriff. On March 31, 1894, the treasurer of Rio Grande County issued a tax deed conveying all of the mining claims and improvements of the Little Annie Mining Company to L. W. Winchester.[6]

The Consolidated Gold Mining Corporation was organized under the laws of the State of Colorado May 24, 1893, with a capital of $1 million consisting of 200,000 shares of stock of a par value of $5 a share. Henry S. Hoyt, L. W. Winchester, T. R. Sloan, Alf R. Roach, George Crawford, Marvelle W. Cooper and John L. McNeil were directors.[7]

Theodore N. Barnsdall, as a result of his conversations with A. E. Reynolds, acquired the Consolidated Gold Mining Company, usually called the Consol Gold Mining Company, with the objective of combining his property with Reynolds' Golconda Mining Company. In 1900 Reynolds agreed to combine his company and Barnsdall's Consolidated Gold Mining Company. Eventually that combination, which occurred long after the deaths of both men, gave a single corporation effective control of the Summitville Mining District.[8]

The Consol Gold Mining Company owned the following patented mining claims in 1900: The Little Annie, Golden Queen, Highland Mary, Charles Brastow, Little Ida, Margaretta, and Odin lode claims and the Peterson placer claim that made up the Little Annie Group of Mines.[9]

By 1900 the Little Annie group of mines had been developed by 8,000 feet of drifts, tunnels, raises and shafts on and connecting the Chandler, Ida, French, Montroy, and Winchester Tunnel Levels.[10]

After all the rich oxidized ores had been exhausted, considerable effort was made to develop a process or processes for the treatment of the lower grade sulfide ores. Treatment of the sulfide ores by stamps and amalgamation, as was done for the oxidized ore, was not successful. Arsenic and sulfur from the sulfide ore reacted with the mercury and thus greatly reduced gold and silver recoveries. Chlorination and cyanidation processes were tried and failed.[11]

In its March 3, 1899 issue, the *Denver Times* reported that Dan Kirby, manager of the Consol Gold Mining Company property at Summitville, was in Denver. Kirby was quoted as stating that the company was building a new 60-ton roaster that would be put into operation in May and that there were twenty-five men at work in Summitville. The crew was to be increased to seventy-five or 100 by June.

Unfortunately, the roaster was not put into operation. A Mr. Best of Denver had convinced the company to treat the ore using his secret "Best's Hydrazene Process;" and the company erected the "Best Roaster" and other equipment required for ore treatment, which consisted of crushing and then roasting the ore with Best's patented salt. Subsequently the gold was to be extracted by stamp amalgamation and the copper was to be extracted from the pulp and precipitated on scrap iron. A several-day trial run proved that Mr. Best's process did not work, and the roaster and allied equipment were abandoned.[12] The "Best Process" was the last effort to treat the sulfide ores until the flotation process proved successful many years later. However, ore having a value of $112,117 was produced in 1900.[13]

The American Concentrator Company of Joplin, Missouri tested Summitville ore in 1902 at A. E. Reynolds' request, but they did not come up with an effective method of treatment. John Philip Schuch, vice president and general manager of the Hartford Gold Extraction Company, claimed he could successfully extract gold from the Summitville ore using a cyanide process. However, problems within the Hartford Company prevented Schuch from erecting and operating a mill at Summitville. Reynolds cancelled the experiment and leased the property, hoping royalties would cover expenses.[14]

The Panic of 1907 complicated Reynolds' mining ventures and negatively affected Barnsdall's fortune. It ended plans Barnsdall had developed with Reynolds that would pay for combining the Golconda and Consolidated mining properties at Summitville.[15]

George H. Garrey in his *Report on Summitville Mines, Rio Grande County, Colorado*, February 1948, stated that the Summitville mines were idle from 1900 until the Withrow and Warr Lease from August 1911 to November 1912. Approximately 253 tons of shipping ore were hand-mined during the lease period and had an average assay value of 3.65 troy ounces of gold per ton and produced a net smelter return of $18,597. About 98 tons of this ore was from the sulfide zone and it had an average assay value of 1.04 troy ounces of gold, 8.73 troy ounces of silver, and 17.8 percent copper.

Lessees on the Golconda Mine made a seventeen-ton shipment of gold ore to the Leadville smelter in 1923[16]; and, in 1924, fifteen tons were produced and shipped to the smelter.[17] A small shipment of ore containing gold, silver and lead was shipped in 1925.

In 1926, the estates of Theodore N. Barnsdall and A. E. Reynolds combined their properties to form a single corporation that took effective control of the Summitville Mining District long after the deaths of Barnsdall and Reynolds. Reynolds' Golconda Mining Company and Barnsdall's Consolidated Gold Mining Company were combined into the Summitville Mines Corporation, with the successors to the Barnsdall and Reynolds estates, the Barnsdall Corporation, and Reynolds-Morse Corporation, each owning half of the enterprise.[18]

A lease given to Judge Jessie C. Wiley and John W. "Jack" Pickens in 1926 by the Barnsdall and Reynolds estates just prior to the formation of the Summitville Mines Corporation ended Summitville's slow times.

Summitville – 1926
Courtesy of the Monte Vista Historical Society

CHAPTER 4
REBIRTH
1926-1949

The mining of extremely rich gold ore from Pickens' Cut eventually led to Summitville's rebirth. However, its rebirth was greatly assisted by the U. S. Government increasing the price of gold in 1934 and the development of metallurgy to process Summitville ores efficiently. Summitville mining essentially ceased during World War II after the U.S Government's War Production Board stopped gold mining. The mines, mills, and mining companies of the period are described in this chapter. In addition, an interesting story about the arrest and sentencing of high-graders in 1938 and the portrayal of the town and life in camp depicting what it was like in Summitville leading up to mid-century.

The years 1926 through 1949 were Summitville's most productive, at least in terms of jobs provided and the camp's stability. Summitville was Colorado's leading producer of gold from 1934 through 1942. Metals production for the period was 144,581 troy ounces of gold, 424,286 troy ounces of silver, 46,298 pounds of copper, and 54,521 pounds of lead.

In 1934 the U. S. government decided to dramatically increase its holdings of gold and silver to back its currency. President Roosevelt signed the Gold Reserve Act of 1934 into law on January 30, 1934. Under the terms of this act, the Secretary of the Treasury issued regulations for the purchase of gold by the federal government at $35 per troy ounce. For many years the price of gold had been set at $20.67. The Silver Act of 1934 required the Secretary of the Treasury to purchase silver in large quantities to dramatically increase the government's stockpile of silver. The legislation was enacted by Congress on June 13, 1934 and signed by President Roosevelt on June 19, 1934. The average price of silver in New York had been 35 cents per troy ounce in 1933. American silver producers would receive 64.64 cents per troy ounce from December 21, 1933 to April 10, 1935. The "pegged" price of silver was almost twice 1933's average price. These dramatic price increases for gold and silver fueled Summitville's rebirth.

The rebirth of the district started with a bang shortly before the increase in gold and silver prices, when a mining operation that started with a small open cut called the Pickens' Cut exploited a fantastically rich, but relatively small, ore body.

Pickens' Cut

Pickens' Cut was described in a 1936 Colorado Mining Association article[1]:

Pickens standing where he took out high-grade ore –
July 1929 Photo by Hume, Del Norte
Courtesy of the Rio Grande County Museum, Del Norte, Colorado

The district again came into prominence in 1926 when John W. Pickens and Judge J. C. Wiley secured a lease from the Reynolds-Barnsdall estates and started to mine extremely rich gold ore from a surface exposure about 150 feet northwest of the old Del Norte tunnel [Picken's Cut]. *Between August 26, 1926 and November 19, 1930, the Wiley-Pickens lease shipped 690 tons of ore having a total gross value of $477,939.68 or an average value of $692.67 per ton. In addition they shipped 174 tons from a sublease with a gross value of $19,821.74 and additional small shipments in 1931which brought the total production of the Pickens-Wiley lease to approximately $500,000.*

John W. "Jack" Pickens was a miner and prospector who worked at Summitville and lived in Del Norte with his wife Clara and nine children. District Judge Jessie C. Wiley, his wife Mary, and six children were also residents of Del Norte.

John Wesley Pickens was born in 1869 at Jonesboro, Tennessee. He joined the U. S. Army at the age of eighteen. He then went to Cripple Creek hoping to find his fortune but did not. He went to Summitville in 1893 where he prospected and worked for the various mining companies.[2]

Judge Wiley was born May 22, 1869 in Irving, Illinois. He arrived in Del Norte in 1897 where he served as mayor from 1908 to 1914. He was appointed District Judge in 1914 and served until his death on September 4, 1930.

The story of Pickens' Cut starts at a much earlier time than 1926. During the summer of 1902, Jack Pickens was walking on a trail across the Little Annie property owned by the Barnsdall estate. He noticed an unusual rock in a slide area along a steep section of the trail beneath a prominent butte, later called the "Cliff of Gold." He broke off a piece of the rock and inside he found free gold. He determined that the rock had to have eroded from the butte. He searched the steep hillside many times and accidentally located a fabulously rich outcrop of gold ore. One day while on his lunch hour he climbed the steep hill to search for the source of the unusual rock and had started down to the trail when the slide rock moved under his feet and he lost his balance. He grabbed a low branch of a tree to stop himself from following the rock down the slope. While getting up he discovered that

Judge Jesse C. Wiley
Courtesy of the Rio Grande County Museum, Del Norte, Colorado

the branch he held onto covered an outcropping of gold ore. He covered up the outcrop and put the branch back over it to hide its existence. He then went back to his job at the mine. Pickens kept his find a secret for over twenty-four years hoping to get a lease on the property, but to no avail. He returned to his find annually to make sure it was still hidden.[3]

Judge Jessie C. Wiley helped Pickens secure a five-year lease, 1926 through 1931, on all of the mining properties owned by the Barnsdall and Reynolds estates, including Pickens' Cut, presumably because of a pending law suit between the Commodore and Bachelor Mines at Creede to be held under Judge Wiley's jurisdiction. The Reynolds people felt that the issuance of the lease would influence Judge Wiley to rule in favor of the Commodore Mining Company, owned by the Reynolds estate. The lease should have raised questions of conflict of interest on the part of Judge Wiley but did not. The Commodore Mining Company claimed that mining on the Bachelor property encroached onto the adjoining Commodore property and the Bachelor operation had illegally taken 5,000 tons of ore valued at $200,000 in 1922 and 1923.

Judge Wiley was in no hurry to reach a decision. He rendered a judgment in the district court in Creede on September 23, 1929 in favor of the Commodore Mining Company. By asking for a lease on the Reynolds property, Wiley also gave Bradish Morse the opportunity to arrange the long-delayed merger of the Reynolds and Barnsdall interests into the Summitville Mines Corporation.[4]

Ben Poxson, a well-known mining entrepreneur and public servant, had these comments about Judge Wiley's securing the lease:

Well, this Jack Pickens was pretty smart in a way. He figured that Brad Morse, Reynolds' son-in-law, was kind of the head of things then for the Morse Corporation. He devised a scheme whereby he would get Judge Wiley to ask for a lease on Summitville. The two of them were old personal friends, just a couple of old timers, you know. Wiley figured that the Reynolds people couldn't turn him down because he was hearing this $200,000 case. Well, the lease was granted to Wiley and Pickens. I was clerk of the district court at that time.[5]

After the lease was signed, Wiley asked Pickens how much money would be required to extract the gold. Pickens answered: "*About forty cents, a lard bucket and a tack hammer will make both you and I rich.*" Pickens took Wiley to Summitville and showed him the "Cliff of Gold." He knocked off a sample of the outcropping gold ore with his hammer and showed it to Wiley. Wiley said: "*Jack, am I dreaming or is this fairyland?*"[6]

Pickens, his son Cecil, and other miners immediately went to work after the lease had been let. Before the winter snows arrived, they mined twenty-two tons of gold ore worth $102,000 from an excavation [Pickens Cut] sixteen feet deep into the ore shoot. The ore shoot itself was twelve feet in diameter and vertical. Before the winter snows arrived, supplies were stored at camp and the men worked all winter opening up the ore shoot by a tunnel some seventy feet below the surface outcrop located by Pickens in 1902. The tunnel, driven many years prior, barely missed the rich ore shoot. An ore shoot is a columnar ore body on a vein where it is intersected by a crossing fault or another vein. A second tunnel some 155 feet below the outcrop also came close to the ore shoot and provided access to it for Pickens and his crew. No ore was shipped until July because of deep snow.[7]

Ben Poxson described the mining operation in his reminiscences:

The original Pickens open cut wasn't very much deeper than from the ceiling to the floor of a room, and not very big around. But, they took out $503,000. There was a little ore shoot that started to surface at a place where you couldn't tell what it was. All he had to start with was about ten or eleven feet exposed on the surface. Then he got down a little ways and it lengthened out a little bit, but they had to mine it six feet wide in order to take the ore out. In order to get the ore, they moiled down on the ore. It was quite a difficult job of mining that rich ore. They'd go down the length of their moil, load the holes with powder, cover it all over with old blankets and quilts, and then shoot it. It would bump up under these blankets, but it wouldn't get away from them. Then they'd take the blankets off, gather up the ore and then go down. They followed that vein down. It averaged about ten feet in length, but it went down 60 feet, at which point the high grade ore played out. In the little ten foot long shoot, the vein was real narrow, but they had to mine it six feet in order to work on it.[8]

V. W. "Bill" Ellithorpe's father and uncle were two of the miners who worked for Jack Pickens. Bill's Uncle Ralph wrote a book about Summitville's history entitled *Poker, Politics and Gold*. Bill's recollections of what his father, Uncle Ralph, and Aunt Adalenore told him regarding Jack Pickens, and of his childhood memories of that time, follow[9]:

Jack Pickens worked for the A. E. Reynolds company for five or six years prior to the time Judge Wiley leased the property. Aunt Adalenore told me that she would see Jack walking to Judge Wiley's house in the winter with gunnysacks wrapped around his shoes. He did not have enough money to buy overshoes.

Evidently there was a riff between Pickens and Reynolds. It is not explicit to what caused this riff, but the Reynolds company would not give Jack a lease on the property he wanted.

The first high-grade ore out of the Jack Pickens workings was put in a 50-gallon barrel with the lid welded on. That barrel of ore brought $60,000. Aunt Adalenore said part of the deal between Jack and Judge Wiley was that they would both pay all their debt. She thought Judge Wiley had a lot more debt than Jack, but the agreement was not made on a dollar and cent basis. Each man would just pay his bills. Aunt Adalenore thought Jack got the short end of the deal. I was eight or nine years old at the time of all this excitement. I remember Jack riding about in a beautiful Pierce Arrow automobile. Dad and Uncle Ralph were working for Jack at this time. They stayed at the old Bowen house. Uncle Ralph told me that the second shipment of ore was kept in the old Bowen house. He said they piled the ore underneath the window, and when you looked at the pile from across the room, it had a yellow gold appearance as the sun struck it through the window. Jack gave my Uncle Ralph and my dad each a small gold specimen when they worked for him.

I remember seeing an old Model T truck coming down the Piños Creek road. I do not think that an old Model T could come up to Summitville, and therefore, I think that this ore was hauled by a team and wagon to what was called Tollgate, a station between Del Norte and Summitville. Then they transferred it to the Model T truck.

Uncle Ralph told me that no dynamite was used to mine ore from the Pickens' workings. The mining was done with single jacks and moils.

Although the Poxson and Ellithorpe accounts disagree on whether "powder" as the miners called dynamite was used or not used, they agree that mining was done by hand tools. A moil is a short section of drill steel about one inch in diameter sharpened on one end. The sharpened end is driven into the ore with a "single jack" hammer. There were two sizes of hammers used by early miners – the single jack, weighing four pounds, on a short handle for use by one hand; and a double jack, weighing eight pounds, on a long handle for use of both hands.

*Free Gold Specimen from Pickens' Cut
Courtesy of V. W. "Bill" Ellithorpe*

  According to Ralph Ellithorpe's book, he and Judge Wiley visited Jack Pickens and were shown into a small room where the floor was covered by canvas. In the center of the room was a pile of high grade gold ore glittering like golden jewelry. The next morning this ore was double sacked in canvas bags and then taken to the Wiley residence in Del Norte. About twenty tons of lower grade ore was hauled by wagon to Del Norte and stored in a warehouse near the railroad tracks. Both the high-grade and lower-grade ore were shipped by rail to the Omaha smelter. Five sacks of high-grade ore were dumped into a steel barrel with a lid welded onto it. The barrel, accompanied by Judge and Mrs. Wiley and Jack, was first shipped to Denver. It was then shipped under guard to Omaha where metallurgist Frank L. Shaw assayed it. The barrel contained 269 pounds of ore that was valued at $62.28 per pound. The lower grade ore was assayed at a little less than $3,000 per ton.[10] Gold at that time was valued at $20.65 per troy ounce.

  Pickens and Wiley also shipped ore to the Golden Cycle Mill in Colorado Springs, Colorado in 1927 and 1928.[11]

The author was assigned as a draftsman to the Post Engineer's office at Camp Carson, Colorado in the spring of 1955 for the last months of his time in the military service. A civilian engineer in the office, named Charlie, had worked for the Golden Cycle Corporation at their Colorado Springs mill during the 1920s and 30s. He was on duty at the mill one Sunday morning when a black Buick touring car arrived at the mill office. Two men stepped out of the car and asked if Golden Cycle could process some gold ore for them. Their names were Jack Pickens and Judge Wiley from Del Norte. Charlie told them that their ore could be processed on a custom basis. Jack and Judge Wiley then delivered their ore shipment – sacks of ore in the back of their automobile. Charlie said he had never seen ore so rich. In fact, the ore was processed in the mill's sampling circuit instead of the regular process because of its richness and small volume.

After the high-grade ore had been exhausted, the value of the remaining ore in Pickens' Cut could not support mining and wagon transportation costs from Summitville to Del Norte, let alone freight to the smelter and smelting costs. Wiley and Pickens made preparations to form a company to erect and operate a cyanide mill to process the lower-grade ore. They asked for a ten-year extension of their lease. Before the plan could be implemented, Wiley died of cancer in September 1930 and Pickens would not continue the partnership with Mrs. Wiley. This meant that the Summitville district would be dormant until the Pickens-Wiley lease expired in June 1931.[12]

Summitville Mines Corporation

The Summitville Mines Corporation was organized in 1926 with the Barnsdall Corporation and the Reynolds-Morse Corporation each owning half. Bradish Morse retained geologist George H. Garrey prior to the expiration of the Pickens-Wiley lease to make a thorough investigation and determine the potential of the Summitville Mines Corporation's property. The investigation showed that Summitville would support future mining operations and provide a large return on investments required to develop the mines and construct and operate a concentrating mill that would cost no less than $300,000. The mill would reduce ore shipment and smelting costs.[13]

Bradish Morse died from a heart attack at home in Denver on December 27, 1931. After her husband's death, Anna Reynolds Morse managed the affairs of the Reynolds-Morse Corporation as president. She was recognized by the Colorado Mining Association as an outstanding mine owner in 1937.[14] Anna Morse married George H. Garrey in 1938.

Garrey was born in Reedville, Wisconsin in 1875. He went to the University of Chicago and graduated in 1898. After teaching school for two years, he returned to the University of Chicago for an advanced degree in geology where he also was an assistant to Alonzo Stagg, one of football's greatest coaches. He then attended the Michigan College of Mines for two years and earned the degree of Engineer of Mines in 1904. He went to work at the U. S. Geological Survey and later joined the American Smelting & Refining Company. He opened a consulting and engineering firm in 1911 and became associated with Colorado mining properties, particularly those owned by the Reynolds-Morse Corporation.

The Summitville Mines Corporation owned most of the mining property at Summitville but was not involved in actual mine operations. The property, consisting of more than one hundred mining claims, was leased out to operating companies, and Summitville Mines Corporation received royalties from the operators.

Mines, Mills and Operating Companies

In July 1933 Benjamin T. Poxson and George H. Garrey organized Summitville Gold Mines, Inc. to lease the claims worked by Pickens and Wiley.[15] The company, with B. T. Poxson as president, cleaned out several old tunnels and performed mine development, specifically 100 feet of drift and 100 feet of raise that year.[16] A small amount of gold and silver was produced. The operation employed ten to fifteen miners.

Benjamin T. Poxson was a well-known business and political figure in Colorado. He was a public servant, a miner, banker, an aide to several Colorado governors, and a friend of many important people in the state. He was born June 12, 1893 in Jackson, Michigan and moved to Alamosa, Colorado in 1914 as a teacher. He was the principal of the Alamosa high school in 1915 and began his career in public service when William "Billy" Adams, the "cowboy governor of Colorado," appointed him to fill a postmaster vacancy in Alamosa. After two years as postmaster, he moved to Denver to be Governor Adams' secretary, actually performing the work of governor, except for signing bills, while Adams was ill and incapacitated. Poxson served as the head of the Colorado Industrial School for Boys in Golden, president of the Colorado Mining Association, chairman of the Colorado Home for Dependent Children, and chairman of the Colorado Racing Commission for many years.[17]

When it became obvious that more capital was required to construct a concentrating mill, develop an efficient mining operation, and provide housing and services for miners and their families, Summitville Consolidated Mines, Inc., a new company with access to the required capital, was formed in April 1934. Poxson and Garrey surrendered their leases and equipment to the new company for one-fifth of its capital stock. F. R. Smith, president of A. O. Smith Corporation of Milwaukee, Wisconsin, a manufacturer of automobile frames and other steel products, controlled Summitville Consolidated Mines, Inc.[18]

Summitville Consolidated Mines, Inc. was immediately provided capital to construct facilities for mining on a large scale. A November 1, 1934 letter from B. T. Poxson, president of the Summitville Gold Mines, Inc., to George Garrey stated the following:

A one hundred ton combination flotation and cyanidation mill, a forty-six mile improved auto and truck highway, a main twenty-six mile electric power transmission line to supply 23,000 volts to our mines and mill, camp power and light lines, mine machinery installations, adequate bunk and boarding houses for present operations, an office and warehouse building, an aerial tram line, an assay and metallurgical office, a trunk telephone line, camp telephone lines, and other facilities necessary for the active operation of the entire properties of the Summitville Mines Corporation, the owners, have been completed and the mill has been tested and the mill and mines at Summitville, Colorado are now in operation by the SUMMITVILLE CONSOLIDATED MINES, INC.

According to the 1934 Summitville report to the Colorado Bureau of Mines and the Colorado Bureau of Mines 1934 annual report, the Little Annie, Reynolds, Iowa, Golconda and other claims were worked on a small scale all year, but the 100-ton flotation and cyanide mill was not completed until October 20, 1934. However, the mill was operating near its capacity and making a high rate of recovery at the end of the year. The aerial tramway, one-half mile in length, connected the Iowa Mine and the new mill. Roads to the Chandler, French, Winchester and Iowa Mines were built, and the Iowa Tunnel was cleaned out and rails installed.

The Reynolds Tunnel was rehabilitated as the main haulage tunnel and provided access to the mine workings that included a connecting raise between the Iowa Tunnel and the Reynolds Tunnel, which was 540 feet below the Iowa.[19]

Summitville – January 31, 1935
Courtesy of Charles A. Harbert

Wightman Fork Road
Courtesy of Charles A. Harbert

Truck Used to Haul Concentrates to and Supplies from Monte Vista /
Wayne Talley - Driver
Courtesy of V. W. "Bill" Ellithorpe

The Summitville Annual Report for 1935 states that the president of Summitville Consolidated Mines, Inc. was L. L. Warriner. Edward Thornton was the general superintendent. The only other mining operation in the district in 1934 was on the Esmond claim. It produced a single car of gold ore that was shipped to the Golden Cycle Mill.[20]

Until 1934, the only access to Summitville was the road from Del Norte that was nearly impassable except during the late summer and fall months. Then, the Civilian Conservation Corps, under U. S. Forest Service supervision, rebuilt the road up the Alamosa River past Jasper to Stunner and then over Stunner Pass to Platoro. The federal Project Works Administration and Rio Grande County constructed a road up Wightman Fork, connecting the newly rebuilt Alamosa River road and Summitville. These roads provided for access and truck haulage to Monte Vista, forty-six miles distant.[21]

B. O. Benson described Summitville in the Colorado Mining Association's 1935 Annual Yearbook:

The year 1935 will long be remembered as the year that Summitville came back. A little more than a year ago, the Summitville Consolidated Mines, Inc. started the revival by putting one of the old properties back in production. Since then the company has erected seventy modern homes for workmen, a school, a warehouse, compressor houses, a machine shop, two mess halls, the post office and numerous other buildings. A mill was built to handle 150 tons of ore a day, but its size had to be doubled, and the newly enlarged 300-ton mill began operations only a few days ago. Several hundred thousand dollars have been spent on a new highway to Monte Vista. Forty pupils and two teachers are using the schoolhouse.

The Iowa Tunnel produced most of the gold ore from the district in 1935. The Reynolds Tunnel rehabilitation had been suspended and the Iowa to Reynolds raise had not been completed.[22] About 4,000 tons of ore were produced and processed each month in 1935 and an average of 135 men were employed. The ore occurrences were spotty and the ore, a mixture of oxides and sulfides, was difficult to treat. Even so, good recovery was attained.[23] The cyanide circuit was not working in late 1935 and, therefore, mill production of 300 tons per day could not be sustained. Mill concentrates were sent to the Leadville smelter.[24] The mill's capacity was reduced in the spring of 1936 from 300 to 150 tons per day by eliminating the mill's flotation sections' 250- ton-per-day middling circuit. "Middling" is the term given to a flotation product containing valuable and waste rock or non-desirable mineral particles normally recycled to reclaim the valuable particles. In this case the "middling" had been sent to the cyanide unit where it was processed, but with considerable loss of the gold and silver values due to its sulfide mineral content that reacted adversely with the cyanide. The 150-ton mill's flotation

Summitville Mill – circa 1935
Courtesy of Charles A. Harbert

tailings were sent to the cyanide unit that was increased in capacity from sixty to seventy tons per day to 150 tons per day by adding tank capacity to the circuit. The cyanide tailings were the only final waste product from the mill and had less than 0.07 troy ounces of gold per ton. [25]

The mill tailings were retained in Wightman Fork by a series of dams. In 1937, three dams were located just below the mill and four were located within a mile downstream from the mill. Water quality in the Alamosa River was impacted by pollution from Alum and Iron Creeks to a great extent, and the additional pollution from the milling operation on Wightman Fork was considered not important.[26]

In 1935 the Summitville Consolidated Mines, Inc. was accused of encroaching on the Esmond claims. B. T. Poxson, in a letter to George H. Garrey dated September 17, 1935, stated that he was negotiating for a lease on the Esmond claims and had made them a proposition they were considering. Most likely Poxson's proposition was accepted.

Ralph C. Ellithorpe, in 1932 to 1934, had a lease on the south half of the Aztec claim that contained a pocket of high-grade ore. The Summitville Consolidated Mines, Inc. drifted over to

Tailings Pond and Summitville Camp in the Background – 1930s
Courtesy of the Rio Grande County Museum

his high-grade and mined it. The following summer the company contested the claim survey. Even though, in 1936, the New Aztec Mining Company filed suit against Summitville Consolidated and its owners for a million dollars in damages for trespass on their ore bodies. Early in 1937, Summitville Consolidated purchased the Aztec claim adjoining the Little Annie group and ended the New Aztec Mining Company's apex suit.[27]

In 1936, the mining operations were conducted through the tunnels at the various mines on the Tewksbury, Annie, Black Wonder, Odin-Dexter, Highland Mary and Pickens veins.[28]

H. F. Detrick was president of Summitville Consolidated Mines in 1937.[29] Detrick, an O. A. Smith engineer, first arrived at Summitville in May, 1935.[30]

In 1938, the raise connecting the Iowa and Reynolds Tunnels was completed. Ore was then dropped down to the Reynolds Tunnel for haulage to the mill. In 1939, battery powered locomotives were used in the Reynolds Tunnel, where rails and rolling stock had been installed. Most of the workings were dry due to drainage provided primarily by the Reynolds Tunnel.[31]

Completion of the raise between the Iowa and Reynolds levels fulfilled A. E. Reynolds' plan for mine development when he started the Reynolds Tunnel in 1897. This method provided the cheapest method of ore transportation and also provided ventilation and drainage for the mines. It also made getting supplies to the upper workings easier, particularly in the winter months, and allowed centralizing the work force at one lower camp. Unfortunately, the Reynolds Tunnel had to be shut down much of the time for repairs. Ore was then transported from the Iowa Mine by the aerial tram and by truck from Copper Hill.

Glory hole mining from the surface produced the bulk of the ore during the summer months of 1938 and continued at least to 1940. The method was in use in 1937 as described by Jos. R. Guiteras.[32] First, a raise was driven upwards in the ore vein from the underground workings to the surface to create an ore pass. Then the ore was mined downward. The ore was dropped by gravity through the raise to the underground workings below, where it was then hauled to the mill.

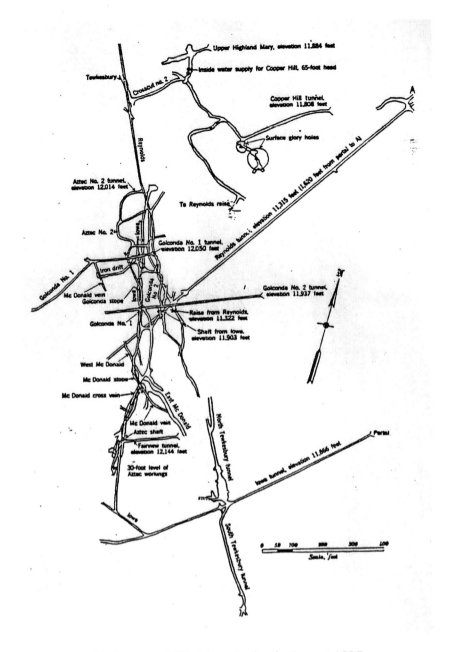

Underground Workings Active in August 1937
U. S. Bureau of Mines Information Circular 6990

In 1938, the mill produced three separate products that were shipped to smelters: high-grade flotation concentrates that contained gold and silver; gold-silver precipitates derived from cyanided flotation tailings; and gold-silver bullion from a small stamp-amalgamation process used to treat high-grade ore.[33]

The mill was revised in 1939. The use of flotation machines and tables were discontinued and a jig was installed in the ball mill circuit to remove high-grade sulfide concentrate that was shipped directly to the smelter. The remainder of the pulp was treated by a cyanide process. The precipitates were smelted at the mine and the bullion shipped to the Denver Mint.[34]

The Narrow Gauge Tunnel was driven in 1940 to intersect the Copper Hill workings and other veins that had surface showings of ore at a lower elevation.[35] The Iowa, Narrow Gauge, and Reynolds Tunnels were in operation in 1941. The Reynolds Tunnel was equipped with a new rail haulage system its entire length. The old rails were deteriorated by acid water while the tunnel was inactive. However, the rail was reported to be in good repair in 1939.[36]

Summitville Mill – circa 1940
Courtesy of Charles A. Harbert

Ore Dump and Mine Road
Courtesy of the Monte Vista Historical Society

There was no mining during 1941, either on the Barnsdall Oil Company property or the Esmond claims. The entire production was from the Reynolds-Morse property.[37]

A copper ore body was discovered and was actively being developed in 1942. A tunnel driven for transportation purposes cut the copper ore zone. The Reynolds Tunnel drained water carrying copper sulfate in solution for many years, and the iron pipes installed years ago in the tunnel were filled with cement copper. Metallurgical tests showed that the copper ore could be processed in the Summitville mill flotation section.[38]

Summitville Consolidated Mines, Inc. operated the mines and mill at Summitville until August 1, 1942, when it relinquished its lease. Gold Links Mining Company got a lease to continue operating the mines and mill throughout the remainder of 1942.[39]

Benjamin. T. Poxson and George H. Garrey owned the Gold Links Mine. The company was originally formed to lease the Gold Links Tunnel at Ohio City in Gunnison County, Colorado.[40]

Gold Links Mine – circa 1943
Courtesy of the Monte Vista Historical Society

The U. S. Government's War Production Board Order L208, issued in 1942 shortly after the start of World War II, mandated that all production of non-essential metals be stopped. This included gold. However, mining and processing of copper ore with minor gold and silver values continued at Summitville at a reduced tonnage under a special grant from the War Production Board. Many of the Summitville miners went to the Climax Molybdenum Mine north of Leadville. Molybdenum was considered a strategic metal. The flotation/cyanidation mill was converted to straight flotation for production of copper for the war effort. A fifty-ton per day stamp and amalgamation mill was used to process the gold and silver ore. The bullion was shipped to the Denver Mint.[41] Some say that Wilfley tables were also used. According to the *Engineering and Mining Journal*, Volume 143, 1942, the first car of copper concentrate was shipped to Salt Lake for smelting. The Narrow Gauge and Reynolds Tunnels gave access to a high-grade copper vein and copper was mined from 1943 into 1945.[42]

Summitville Mill – July 1944
Courtesy of Arlie Stanger

The War Production Board Order L208 was cancelled in 1945 and Summitville returned to primarily mining gold.[43] Gold Links Mine continued its operation until June 20, 1946, when it relinquished its lease. The owner, Summitville Mining Company, operated the property for the remainder of 1946 to October 1947. Mining operations were confined to the lower portion of a block of ore along the so-called Hidden vein. Up to thirty tons per day were mined and treated in the stamp and amalgamation mill section of the mill.[44]

Jones and Nylene from Leadville, Colorado re-opened the flotation section of the Summitville Mill in September 1948 to treat copper-gold ore from surface outcrops and dumps. The concentrate was not shipped in 1948. Underground development resulted in the discovery of another vein of copper ore.[45] Jones and Nylene operated the mine and mill four months in 1949. The ore mined was concentrated in the mill. Mine development amounted to 280 feet of drifts.[46]

The re-birth of Summitville mining started with a bang in 1926, and ended with a whimper in 1949.

High-Grading

"High-grading" is a miner's term for taking high-grade ore or rich concentrates from a mine or mill, smuggling the material off the property, and then selling the gold and silver in the ore or concentrates for personal gain. Miners who in the early days used candles for light and drilled holes with hammers and muscle power for low pay under unsafe conditions felt high-grading was their right. However, mine owners did not agree, particularly after they were forced to improve miners' working conditions. They started prosecuting high-graders. High-grading was a problem at Summitville.

As mentioned in the Preface, the author, as a teen-ager, delivered papers to a man who lived in the neighborhood and, according to local gossip, spent time in prison for high-grading gold from the Summitville Mine. The Summitville Consolidated Mining Company, Inc. suspected someone in the mine was high-grading gold and hired a security company to find out who was involved. To make the story more intriguing, the security company investigator found out who was involved and evidently thought it was such a good deal that he joined them. In time, the perpetrators were found out and three were arrested. One was the investigator. Records of the Twelfth Judicial District Court in Del Norte show that the stories were, in fact, essentially true and they are the basis of the following paragraphs.

H. F. Detrick, president of the Summitville Consolidated Mines, Inc., arranged with Paul Newlon, proprietor of The Western Industrial Service and Investigating Service of Denver, to employ a special investigator to obtain information concerning the theft of high-grade ore and concentrates from the Summitville mining operation. An investigator was employed from December 8, 1937 to November 1, 1939. He did not have the authority to remove or sell any ore, concentrates, precipitates or other property stolen from the mining company by any person whatsoever.

The investigator started his investigation by "rustling the mill regularly (seeking employment) and becoming acquainted with a number of the employees," as was reported to his Denver employer. He wrote weekly reports from December 29, 1937 to

October 26, 1939 to Paul Newlon, who forwarded them to H. F. Detrick.

His report of January 15, 1938 stated that a dentist in Monte Vista bought small quantities of high-graded gold for $10 per ounce. Several reports stated that high-graded ore from Summitville was sold to a party in Leadville by different individuals.

The investigator, in his report of March 7, 1938, stated that he was positive the bulk of the high-graded gold was being marketed in Denver. The procedure used to handle the rich ore suggested that someone high up was in on the deal. He said that this could be remedied if more care was used at the mill when the ore was delivered there from the mine where it was sampled. Those sampling the high-grade ore put it into sample sacks, hauled it to the mill where it was allowed to lay around on top of the grizzly (a sloping screen used to separate undersized rock) at the ore bin. This location was very easy to get to by anyone in camp. He stated that most of the loss was taking place in this way and there were several individuals involved. He let it be known to a suspected high-grader that he made trips to Denver frequently and would be willing to accompany him there, hoping that he would take some high-grade with him to sell.

In his report of June 11, 1938, the investigator reported that the deal on the high-grade was coming along slowly, but he had found out that two individuals were in on it. Previously he had said that there were four individuals involved in the high-grading scheme, that it was a "good-sized steal," and that the high-graders wanted top money.

On June 27, 1938, he reported that a rumor that the company had two men checking for high-graders made it hard to get information. His July 26, 1938 report stated that ore was being high-graded and hauled to a farm near Monte Vista.

The July 26, 1938 report stated that one high-grader was taking the high-grade and that another was hauling it down the hill three or four times a week to a farm near Monte Vista. The high-graders told the investigator they had $10,000 worth. The high-grade ore carried between two and three ounces of gold per pound.

On September 26, 1938, the investigator reported that Summitville Consolidated Mines, Inc. wanted to catch the high-grading gang all together, but that, in the meantime, "a lot of valuable stuff was slipping away."

The October 21, 1938 report said the company had made changes. Steel gates were used to close off the high-grade workings. This made unauthorized access to that area almost impossible. A couple of men were at Summitville in July and August trying to buy high-grade. This left the impression that they were company men and this, of course, scared the high-graders.
In his last report made October 25, 1939, the investigator said that at one time he reported there were no organized high-graders but he was convinced that the crusher operators were getting organized and should be watched.

On November 24, 1939, complaints by Edward Thornton, general superintendent, were filed in the Justice Court charging two high-graders and the investigator with taking nine sacks of high-grade gold ore from the Summitville Mine. Rio Grande County Sheriff C. D. Phillips arrested the men for stealing 500 pounds of high-grade gold ore worth $533.00 on or about June 1, 1938. On November 25, 1939 the investigator appeared in court and pleaded not guilty. Since no bond was furnished he was placed first in the Rio Grande County jail and then in the Alamosa County jail. On November 28, 1939, the high-grader who transported the gold ore to Monte Vista appeared in court and was released after his bond was posted.

The other high-grader and the investigator were indicted for grand larceny and convicted on December 13, 1939 by Judge Palmer of the 12th Judicial District Court. The high-grader was sentenced to no less than eighteen months and no more than three years in the Colorado State Penitentiary. The investigator was sentenced to a minimum of six years and no more than ten years. The convicted high-grader's co-workers and residents of Summitville petitioned the judge and district attorney to show clemency to this young man with a family who has erred. The petitioners, 186 of them, said the high-grader had always conducted himself well, taken care of his family, and had been a steady worker.

In a statement made to Sheriff Phillips and Chief of Police Richardson, the high-grader said he had worked at Summitville for five years and that he lived at Summitville with his wife and kids. He stated that about May 1st, the other high-grader talked him into taking some high-grade ore. He carried out eight to ten sacks of ore, a few at a time so they wouldn't be missed. The other high-grader then loaded the sacks into his car and took them down the hill. This occurred at 10 to 11 p.m. for twelve to fourteen nights covering about four months. The total number of sacks of high-grade ore was sixty to eighty. The other high-grader told him that the investigator was to dispose of the ore.

The investigator stated that on or about June 18, 1938 he hauled and disposed of nine sacks of high-grade ore taken from Summitville in Denver. He received $533.00 for the stolen ore. He gave the high-graders about $400.00 and kept the rest for himself. He then made a second trip to Denver on June 25 and sold twelve more sacks for about $500 that he converted to his personal use. These sacks of ore were also stored near Monte Vista. During the trial, the Court stated, in its opinion, the investigator was employed to prevent the very thing he promoted and that he double-crossed the company for which he worked, the mining company, and those with whom he co-operated.

Life in Summitville

Summitville was the second largest mining camp in Colorado in 1935, with a population of 700. While another source puts Summitville's population at 518 people in 1935, including more than 300 miners and mill men;[47] Summitville's greatest population was estimated to be fifteen hundred, with about nine hundred men on the company's payroll.[48]

The Summitville Consolidated Mining Company, Inc. erected seventy modern homes, bunkhouses, mess halls, a bathhouse, an amusement hall, two-room school, post office, a commissary and a municipal water system. Summitville was a company town and, therefore, there is no official record of it in the Colorado Division of State Archives and Public Records. None of the homes or facilities were owned by anyone other than the mining company. The company houses generally contained two rooms, with tarpaper on the outside of the one-by-twelve inch wood plank walls and Celotex on the inside. They were heated by pot-bellied coal and wood stoves, which were constantly in use during the long winter months. The houses had running water and electricity, but there were no sewers so the toilet was an outside two-holer in a wooden shack. Baths were taken in a washtub and the bath water was heated on the stove. The bath water was then carried outside for disposal.

Summitville Houses – 1935
Courtesy of Charles A. Harbert

Life in Summitville was not easy at an elevation of over 11,000 feet. Tremendous snowfall and limited transportation to and from the camp made living difficult, particularly during the long winter months. There were no saloons in Summitville, quite unlike most mining camps. Occasionally a dance was held at the boarding house and liquor for the dance was brought up from the San Luis Valley. Other than those occasional dances, listening to the radio, card playing, fishing, skiing or snowshoeing were the common recreational activities. Minnie Hanks, who taught school at Summitville in the mid-1940s, said the miners skied down the power line right-of-way to Del Norte for a weekend

Bunkhouse at Summitville
Courtesy of the Rio Grande County Museum

Summitville Houses, 1930
Courtesy of Charles A. Harbert

Post Card From Summitville
Courtesy of Charles A. Harbert

Post Office Interior with Kenneth Stanger,
Postmaster, at Window
Courtesy of Charles A. Harbert

The Company Store
Courtesy of the Rio Grande County Museum

School House with Students Skiing off Roof
Courtesy of the Rio Grande County Museum

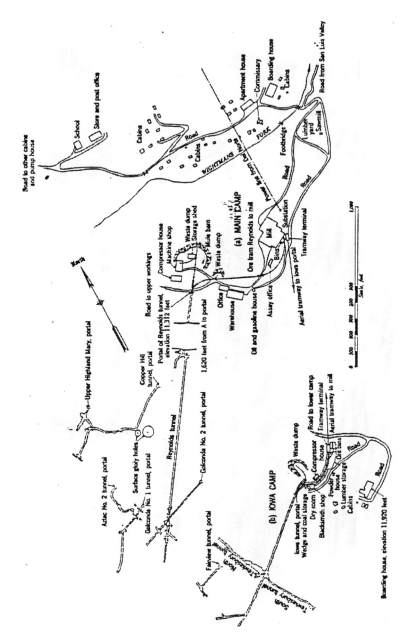

Surface Plans Showing Buildings at (a) Main Camp and (b) Iowa Camp
U. S. Bureau of Mines Information Circular 6990, August 1938

when "cabin fever" got bad. A company nurse provided simple medical care and a company doctor from Alamosa made trips to Summitville and was available to the employees and their families.

The post office at Summitville was the highest in the land at 11,500 feet. It opened July 12, 1935, closed in 1942, reopened in 1944, and closed in November 1947.

The following descriptions of life in Summitville are from individuals who lived there during the 1930s and 1940s. The Rio Grande County Museum recorded their oral interviews and has them on file.

Living Conditions

Harry Zeiler was a child when his parents went to Summitville in 1935. When they first arrived during the summer rains they lived in a tent. His dad dug a trench through the middle of it to channel water out. Later that fall they moved to one of three cabins within a mile of the mine and a mile from Summitville proper. Harry slept in a rollaway bed that was stored under the main bed. Harry's father had a rope stretched between the house and the Iowa Mine so that he could follow the rope home when the wind blew while he was working nights. Harry had to learn to ski because it was necessary to get to school. He felt there must have been fifteen feet of snow at times. On the way home from school, he put his skis on the tram and rode it uphill to his house.

Robert Myers described the house his family lived in.

Our house when we first moved to Summitville had two rooms. One room was used for the kitchen with one bed for me. The other room was Mom and Dad's bedroom. A two-story addition was built about a year later on the lower side of the house. Mom and Dad used the top room for their bedroom. There was a trap door and steps going down from the added bedroom to my bedroom below.

Martin Gates, who moved to Summitville with his family in 1936, said there were three boardinghouses at the time — one in the main part of the camp, one up by the Iowa and one in Sunnyside. The boarding houses were primarily for single men or men who didn't have their families staying with them.

Entertainment

Harry Zeiler enjoyed the silent movies at the commissary (company store). He remembered seeing a movie there in the wintertime when the snow was half way up to the eaves of the two-story building.

Harriet Parker joined a sewing club that met once a week to sew and play cards.

Robert Myers moved to Summitville in 1935 with his parents when he was in the second grade. They left in 1942. He said they spent most of their time skiing in the winter. The kids skied off the top of the schoolhouse during recess and spun string tops on the schoolhouse floor when the weather was bad and the teachers wouldn't let them outside. There was a Christmas program and nearly all of the kids took part in it. They also put on plays or skits in school during the year. Box suppers and dances were held once in a while in the boarding house. All the tables in the dining room were moved against the walls. The kids all went to the dances with their parents The little kids who didn't dance would just crawl up on the table in a pile of coats and go to sleep.

Martin Gates said there was some alcohol that people brought to the dances, but he didn't remember any big brawls.

Melvin Gates enjoyed fishing on Park Creek or over North Mountain at the head of Beaver Creek.

Medical Care

Martin Gates said there was no regular doctor, but Dr. Donovan came up to Summitville on visits. There was a mine nurse, Mary Jane Carruthers, who would treat the sick or injured. The company had an ambulance – a panel truck. The driver, named Jones, tried to set a record each time he went down to Monte Vista or Alamosa with someone who was sick or hurt.

Police Protection

Harriet Parker said the town had a constable or cop, but he wasn't needed.

Irene Duncan Hutchinson said that Summitville was not a real town – no mayor or police. If a miner got rowdy, the mine superintendent put him in his place and there were lots of miners who would help him and see to it that the miner behaved. Irene said they never had any major problems.

Barney Black moved to Summitville with his family in 1935. He said that the sheriff, if he was needed, was called out of Rio Grande County but as far as anyone at Summitville knew, there was never a need. There were a few deputized people out of the sheriff's office at Summitville. Usually everybody settled their own troubles.

Education

Martin Gates tells about the local school. He was in the third grade when his family moved to Summitville. There was a two-room schoolhouse and two teachers. There were maybe twenty or thirty students in each room. One room held grades one through four. The other room contained grades five through eight. The school was under the Del Norte school system, and the superintendent of school came up about once a year.

Harry Zeiler had a dog, the only dog they'd allow in the schoolhouse. It would come right in and sit by his seat.

Melvin Gates said most of the kids skied to school. After a few trips, the trail was packed and you could walk on top the snow. If there was a blizzard, they'd let the kids out early. His father would take ten or twelve foot two-by-fours and drive them into the ground to mark the trail. In a blizzard no one had any idea where they were going until they fell off the trail. The two by fours helped out a lot.

Working Conditions

Harriet Parker and her husband moved to Summitville in 1938 when he got a job in the mine. He received four dollars a day when he started, and his pay was later raised to $4.25 per day. Working conditions were not good. Water dripped down from above all the time. It "watered" their clothes and shoes. The miners wore rubber boots and diggers (a miners' term for clothes worn during work in the mine) – big canvas pants. Mine work was awful hard on clothes.

    Kathryn Airy Fouquet Davies stated she and her husband were married in 1934 during the depression and had no money, so work at the mine was welcome. There was a clearing up on the mountain where the miners walked to work in the winter. In the summer they took trucks. When they came off shift in the winter, Kathyrn said they looked like little flies against the snow. One night she was watching and saw a man accidentally step off the hardened trail into soft snow and they had to pull him back up. It was her husband. He weighed about two hundred pounds. The miners worked eight-hour shifts. Wages started at $3.50 a day. At the same time, farmers were paying $1.00 per day. They didn't have a washing machine, so they used a tub to wash clothes. Her husband wore his work clothes home and you can imagine what they were like. Kathryn put them on the scrub board and scrubbed them with a brush and then let them drip dry. Occasionally she would ask her husband to bring his diggers home and he'd say, "You don't want to do that." She said bring them home anyway. They'd be coated with mud. He operated a buzzy, a machine that drilled holes for the dynamite. He said he was the only man on the hill that had clean diggers.

    Barney Black told that during his time in the mine a fellow by the name of Red Johnson and he went to work in the mine one day. The big timber that held the ore up near the mine entrance broke and all the ore came down and closed the mine tunnel so no one could go in or out. He and Red spent twelve to fourteen hours in the mine while the tunnel entrance was cleared. It was dark and Barney wanted to dig his way out but they were about a thousand feet underground, so it wasn't possible. The first thing Red did was turn on the buzzy, a rock drill powered by compressed air. They used it for air to breathe. Red said, "We got a free day, so sit down and take life easy." Barney stated that accidents were pretty common in the mine. People got broken legs and other injuries from falling rocks. Some accidents were fairly minor and others pretty major. People were sometimes killed in those accidents. Rock falls, pre-mature explosions of dynamite, and things like that. Barney remembered two major accidents when he was working in the mine. One man was caught in a pre-mature blast and was killed. Another man was caught in a cave-in that hurt him pretty bad.

Bill Ellithorpe remembered an accident involving Gordon Macatee, who was a shift boss at the Iowa. Gordon was pushing a load of timber into the mine. You are not to push a train into a mine. It is against safety regulations. You are supposed to pull it in. The timber hit something and the timber came back and killed Macatee. There was another guy (Wright) who fell off a ladder and down a man-way that was straight up between levels that were fifty feet or more apart. Now the distance between landings can't be over fourteen feet so if you fall you won't fall more than that distance. Ellithorpe sampled the rock on the near vertical sides of glory holes that were open at the surface. He was lowered over the edge in a boson's chair. A scary way to make a living!

Florence McCarty described life in Summitville in her book, *To Catch A Star*, published in 1996:

In the spring of 1903 Dad went to Alamosa and Monte Vista and looked for a permanent job but found none. He inquired about Summitville. Someone said men were being hired to work there. He contacted someone in Summitville and was hired. My parents loaded up the big old wagon with furniture, rocking chairs, center table, big black trunk, bedstead, bedding, the pictures, fancy lamp, silver service and every item they owned and started for a new job. Shep, our dog, was with them and excited as they. In Monte Vista they bought a stock of groceries and went on down the Gunbarrel Road to the road that would follow up the Alamosa River. Near Wightman's Fork, they started up the steep winding road to Summitville. The road was so steep he (Florence's father) *had to reassemble the load to keep it on the wagon. Some portions of the road were so narrow it would have been impossible to get past an oncoming wagon without one vehicle being taken apart and carried past the other. My mother, with one baby on her lap and the other wedged between her and Dad, was apprehensive about one of us slipping off the wagon. There were portions where she demanded to be let off the wagon to walk with the children, and yet she knew if something happened to Dad, being alone in the wild area would be almost worse than death.*

The old house the management designated for our use was built of rough weathered timber. The rooms were large. The peaked roof covered deep insulation of sawdust, which was a blessing. Battens outside the rough vertical boards covered the cracks. Inside there was black tarpaper. Whoever had lived there previously had labored well to make a warm weather-tight house and Dad and Mama were grateful.

They unloaded the wagon and the next morning Dad started work at the mine. There was a bountiful supply of wood. No hauling to be done here. Mama looked at the huge pile, glad there would be no long days of waiting while Dad went to the hills for fuel. All these little details of their lives were given me in later years when they so loved to tell and I to listen.

At the mining office there were extra supplies of canned goods in case anyone ran out. There was a cook at the bunkhouse who cooked for men without wives. Few wives were in camp. Now and then a wagonload of supplies drove into camp.

Summer, there, waned in a hurry. Almost immediately as the summer cooled a bit, yellow leaves showed at timberline. The wind blew off the cold snow patches close to the mine. Washdays ended with wet clothes brought in to dry in the house. Instead of carrying water from the spring, after snows began, it was easier to melt snow for domestic use. There was just no end of snow. It was everywhere. Sometimes one could not see some of the buildings close by. Often the frigid wind blew for days. A person scarcely dared venture out of the door, that is, a woman didn't. Dad had to walk a snow-drifted trail to the mine, but not far. The horses were kept snug in a well-insulated barn close to the house. Near them inside was a mountain of hay that had taken a pile of money to buy. There were also oats. Having a team a whole winter long without any work for them to do was indeed a luxury, but what was to be done with them? Occasionally, if the snow wasn't too deep, someone would rent them for a hauling job.

As to Shep, he seemed to enjoy the winter. His yellow and orange coat grew so thick it was hard to run one's hand through the fur. He was anxious to be out and he tracked game from morning to night. Snowshoe rabbits were available but hard to see in the whiteness of the landscape. Shep could track a rabbit but he failed to kill them. When he cornered one, he looked at Dad, helpless. Maybe he had a kind heart. Who knows?

There were martins and mink, red foxes, coyotes, and near streams there were muskrats. Dad had brought his traps and he laid trap lines and every day after work he went out to check them. He piled the hides in the barn to await a trip to Monte Vista when summer came again.

All in all, the family was contented. Carl, then three and one-half, fretted at being indoors so much. Heavily-clothed, he spent endless hours at the frosted windows trying to see a bird or rabbit. I'm sure I was contented enough. I was about one and a half years old. I was walking very well and Mama said she had her hands full keeping me out of trouble, away from the hot stove and away from frosted windows, and erect instead of playing on the splintery floors. I must have grown pale from the lack of sunshine.

Dad worked seven days a week all winter. There was nothing to do on Sunday except stay inside. Some of the men played cards, but Dad never did this in his life. As the winter waned a bit and it was nice to get out for as bit of fresh air he began making trips around the area to prospect. By that time, men were off Sundays as they liked to get out if there was something to do and no snow blowing.

There were blizzards in March and the poor shack trembled and moaned. Mama wondered if the wind would ever stop. April wasn't much better. May seemed to moderate some and one took hope that summer would come again, but instead, there was more snow. June arrived, finally, and trees were budding and one could see down the mountain to lower altitude.

Dad left his job in Summitville in early July. They loaded up the wagon and went on down the precarious road to the Alamosa River, then drove to the ghost town of Stunner. Dad found an empty cabin and they moved in.

The following descriptions of life in Summitville are from two individuals who lived in Summitville during the 1930s and 1940s and were interviewed by the author.

Arlie Stanger lived at Summitville from 1938 to 1942. Her husband Kenneth was postmaster, her brother-in-law Herb had the store, and her father-in-law Frank Stanger was the mining company's auditor. Her stories about Summitville in her own words and pictures follow[49]:

Snow Tunnel to Door of Store and Post Office

Arlie Stanger on Skis

There were four or five large buildings in camp. The smallest building housed the store, the post office and a back storage room with a small pot-bellied stove that heated the water. Upstairs, Herb and Bette Stanger had a two-room apartment. Also there were three small bedrooms and a bathroom — what a luxury — on the second floor. My husband Kenny built a two-room apartment for us across the front of the building so we had four big windows. When the snow piled up we could see the whole camp. Downstairs they had to shovel a tunnel from the front door to where the snowplow ended the road. Across the tailings pond was the big office building with apartments upstairs. Between were the boarding house and an apartment building.

There was a perfect hill for skiing just above the store. We would laboriously climb to the top and then ski down the hill making the effort of climbing the hill worthwhile.

Man on Snowdrift on Second Story Above the Store

One moonlit night we soaked some old brooms in kerosene, lit them for torches and skied down the hill. Once was enough. One sunny day Kenny and I got a ride to the upper mine so we could ski down. We followed the frozen snow-covered creek. It was a beautiful, quiet ride through the wilderness. People at Summitville used snowshoes and toboggans as well as skis.

The second winter we were there, I taught the four upper grades of the two-room schoolhouse that was a separate building behind the store. The children would get there on skis or on paths that were made by carefully walking in the same place after each snow and marked with tall sticks. Eventually the snow was so deep they could ski off of the schoolhouse roof. I had grades five through eight and ten pupils. It was quite a trick getting every subject in every day but the children were very cooperative.

One winter six or eight of the wives formed a roller skating club. We met in the evening in the dining room (in the bunkhouse) after Molly and the girls had cleaned up. It was fun skating around the tables. Molly was a wonderful cook. We often ate dinner there. We made the most of the short summers.

After all of the snow had melted, one of my adventures was a ride in an ore bucket from the mill in the lower camp to the upper mine and camp. Kenny arranged with the boss for a

Students and Teachers in Front of School House – 1938-39
(Arlie Stanger, left rear, taught classes five through eight, Louise Hanna, right rear, taught classes one through four)

time when the buckets weren't needed. I went in one and Kenny followed in the next. It was a beautiful ride with the little valley far below.

Another treat for me was a trip into one of the mines. As the miners still believed that a woman in the mine was bad luck, we went on a Sunday when most of the miners were not there. Two old mules were grazing in front of the mine. They had been retired when electric mine cars came along. We got into the mine car wearing hats with lights on them. The total darkness was terrifying. A tour of the mill was very interesting, too. It was huge.

In such a small community we knew everyone and made good friends, some of whom we kept in touch for years after the mine closed and we all had moved on. Living in the camp was rugged but always interesting. I might add that Dad Stanger was the company auditor. He and his wife were a remarkable older couple who enjoyed life. In the winter they got around on snowshoes and walked over to the boarding house for dinner plus taking short hikes.

There were whispers of gold smuggling. (Both Arlie Stanger and her father-in-law Frank signed the petition to the Court for clemency for one of the high-graders who was sentenced for smuggling.)

Raylene McWilliams Owen, a retired biology teacher, spent her early childhood in Summitville. Her story follows[50]:

Grandfather Kuhn found a job at Summitville in the 1930's as a tinsmith for the mine where he worked for thirteen years until the mine closed. Until recently, many of his roofs and stovepipes could still be seen at Summitville.

Frances Kuhn, his daughter and my mother, taught school in the late 1930's, as did her older sister. Frances lived with her father in one of the cabins furnished by the mining company. When she would go to the boarding house, the miners all became very polite because "the teacher was here." They would vie to lace up her tall boots when she got ready to go back out in the snow.

Frances left Summitville to teach school in Del Norte in 1940. She then married Ray McWilliams. He was drafted in 1942, served during World War II and was discharged in 1945.

Arlie Stanger in Aerial Tram Bucket

He then took his wife and me to Summitville where he was the bookkeeper and payroll clerk from January 1946 to late 1947 when the mine was shut down.

I lived with my parents and baby brother, Eugene, in a second story apartment in the Summitville bunkhouse. The bunkhouse had apartments on the second floor on one end of the building. The mine superintendent and his wife occupied the largest apartment. The apartments had a common bathtub room. The other end of the second floor was filled with rooms for miners. The first floor contained the mine offices and warehouse.

The cook at the boarding house on the other side of the valley was Grover Green who was an alcoholic. When he ran out of whiskey, he would drink the cooking vanilla. He made excellent chili. Grover's recipe for chili follows:

>*1½ pounds of hamburger*
>*fry grease out and brown meat*
>*2 teaspoons salt*
>*medium onion, fine cut*
>*4 or 5 pieces of garlic or garlic salt*
>*1 can tomato paste or can of tomatoes*
>*3 teaspoons chili powder (heaping)*
>*2 teaspoons oregano leaves*
>*add water, boil 30 minutes, simmer, thicken with flour and add beans if desired*

I was especially fond of his red jello. A mule barn not only served mules used around the mine, but also provided a place to raise rabbits that ended up on the boarding house dining room tables.

In order to cross the valley, I remember climbing the steep wooden stairs through the mill, as it was shorter than going around. I passed by the operating cyanide vats, ball mill, and shaker tables. Very scary to a child. During the winter months I went through a snow tunnel to get to the commissary. I remember snow completely covering the first floor of the bunkhouse. Unfortunately, I had no children of my age to play with while living at Summitville.

In the winter of 1946, during a smallpox scare at Summitville my parents took me to the San Luis Valley in their 1939 Chevrolet for a smallpox vaccination. The Wightman Fork road, which was not good under the best of conditions, was made even worse in the winter by mud, ice, and darkness.

I remember fishing trips on a stream, probably the Alamosa River, where my father carried me on his back in his army backpack. On one fishing trip, we met a sheepherder who let me ride his horse. What a thrill!

The following photograph, taken about 1941, shows the Summitville town site looking north toward North Mountain. Across the road are homes and a boarding house built by the A. O. Smith Corporation where employees lived during the 1930s into 1941. The large building on the left is the Bowen House built before the turn of the century. The small outbuilding close to the Bowen House was the latrine – a twelve-holer. Brothers Harry and Ralph Ellithorpe lived in the Bowen House when they worked for Jack Pickens and Judge Wiley in 1928. V. W. "Bill" Ellithorpe lived in the boarding house, the building to the far right. The cook was Mrs. Malahan, who had a beautiful daughter, Ginger.[51]

Summitville Town Site – circa 1941
Courtesy of V. W. "Bill" Ellithorpe

CHAPTER 5
LIMITED PRODUCTION AND EXPLORATION
1950 – 1984

Summitville mining did not survive the shutdown of gold mining in World War II and the inflation that followed. Mining operations were limited during the 1950s. A partnership of companies explored for and mined some copper in the 1960s and exploration for porphyry deposits was prevalent in the mining industry during the 1970s. Porphyry deposits are large low-grade copper or molybdenum deposits. Precious metals were of little interest at this time. Based on their knowledge of Summitville area calderas, exploration geologists did explore for porphyry deposits at Summitville and the Upper Alamosa River Basin. No economical copper or molybdenum deposits were discovered, but a large, low-grade gold deposit was defined. However, none of the exploration companies had any interest in the gold deposit. During ASARCO's exploration, a large boulder containing native gold was found. It quite likely eroded from the outcrop of rich ore in Pickens' Cut. It ultimately was donated to the Denver Museum of Natural History, where it is still on display.

Summitville's first recorded production during this period was small amounts of gold and silver in 1954. There was also minor production of gold and silver in 1955, 1958, and 1971. Copper was produced in 1958, 1971, and 1972. The price of copper was high during the 1960s and 1970s, and Summitville was known to have considerable copper mineralization. Total production for the period 1950 to 1984 was 258 troy ounces of gold, 3, 290 troy ounces of silver, and 427,000 pounds of copper.

Limited Production and Exploration

The Newmont Mining Corporation obtained a lease in 1953 on about 2,000 acres of mining property owned by Benjamin T. Poxson and George Garrey. Newmont performed diamond drilling and geological exploration under the direction of John Livermore, a geologist with the Newmont Exploration Department.[1] No ore was produced by Newmont.

The South Mountain Mining Company, owned by Frank E. Siegfried and W. I. McAtee, operated the Gold Links Mine for thirty days in October and November 1954 under lease from the Reynolds-Morse Corporation. The company produced 19 troy ounces of gold and 7 troy ounces of silver. Some gold was recovered from a cleanup of the Little Annie mill.[2]

The South Mountain Mining Company shipped twenty-one tons of gold-silver ore, produced by spare-time prospecting and mining in October and November of 1965, to the Leadville smelter. This resulted in 28 troy ounces of gold and 4 troy ounces of silver.[3]

The General Minerals Corporation of Grand Junction, Colorado and Dallas, Texas leased the Reynolds-Morse property in late 1955 or early 1956.[4] A contract between the General Minerals Corporation and the Defense Minerals Exploration Administration (DMEA) for exploration for copper and lead on the property was signed in September 1958. Substantial exploration and development work was performed. Over 5,000 feet of tunnels were rehabilitated on the Reynolds, Chandler, Dexter and Iowa levels, and 3,000 feet of diamond drilling was done in the Little Annie and Tewksbury vein area.[5] However, only 6 troy ounces of gold, 14 troy ounces of silver and 10,000 pounds of copper were produced in 1958.

Exploratory and development work continued in 1959. Diamond drilling between the Chandler and Reynolds levels on the Little Annie vein was performed with the assistance of the DMEA. Substantial copper ore in the sulfide zone carrying gold and silver was delineated. John B. "Jack" Rigg was the mine operator for General Minerals.[6] Results of the exploration and development work were not acceptable to General Minerals and the company terminated their lease.

Thirteen miners, three women, and one baby lived in Summitville during the time of General Mineral's work. In 1962, Rigg stated to news reporters that he felt most of the camp's buildings could be made ready for occupancy with little repair. The domestic water system, installed in 1934, was still in good condition in 1962. However, another individual who was knowledgeable about Summitville visited the camp in 1963 and stated that the camp was in worse condition than at the time of Pickens' Cut in 1926.[7]

Benjamin T. Poxson surrendered his one-fourth interest in Summitville to the Reynolds-Morse Corporation for their Commodore properties at Creede on November 1, 1960.[8] The Reynolds-Morse Corporation and Poxson had jointly purchased the Barnsdall Corporation's interest in the 1950s, and it was this one-quarter interest that Poxson exchanged for controlling interest in the Commodore Mining Company.[9]

After General Minerals Corporation terminated their lease, Jack Rigg, the son of a noted doctor in Grand Junction, Colorado, leased the property until the summer of 1963. He had an Office of Minerals Exploration loan and drilled several holes on the northeast side of South Mountain that indicated the presence of ore-grade gold and silver mineralization. Rigg entered politics after his Summitville experience and was the associate director for Offshore Minerals Management for the federal government's Minerals Management Services in the mid-1980s. Charles E. Melbye, a consulting geologist, worked for him at Summitville.[10]

The W. S. Moore Company, a small iron mining company headquartered in Duluth, Minnesota, was looking for mineral deposits throughout the United States in the 1960s. In 1963 the company leased the Reynolds-Morse property after learning about it from Charles Melbye. It conducted exploration and development work during the summer months of 1963 under Melbye's direction. The company was very encouraged by the copper showing at Summitville. Eight men were on the payroll.[11] Exploration and development work under an Office of Minerals Exploration contract was fairly steady in 1964. Core drilling and tunnel work, some 2,500 feet in from the portal, was conducted.[12] W. S. Moore's work continued into 1965 and 1966 and consisted of exploration drilling on the surface and underground cleanup work.[13]

W. S. Moore needed financial backing for their exploration and development work and, as a result, the Union Pacific Mining Company, a division of the Union Pacific Railroad, became a partner at Summitville and at other mining projects in the West. Melbye was chief geologist for the Union Pacific Mining Company. Cleveland-Cliffs, an old-time iron mining company, became the third partner in the Summitville project in 1967. Cleveland-Cliffs had been involved in oil shale development near Grand Junction, Colorado, that was not doing well and they wanted another project.[14]

In 1967, W. S. Moore, Cleveland-Cliffs Iron Company, and the Union Pacific Railroad Company signed a joint venture agreement for work at Summitville.[15] A decision was made by the joint venture to bring the Missionary deposit, located at the foot of South Mountain north of the then-existing gold workings, into production. It had previously been drilled by Newmont in 1953. Additional drilling identified a significant copper mineralized area beneath the surface. Sinking an eight by twenty-four foot shaft to the Missionary ore deposit commenced in December 1967.[16]

Shaft sinking continued in 1968 and some drifting was done. The Arthur G. McKee Construction Company of San Francisco, California commenced construction of a 300 ton per day mill. Cleveland-Cliffs managed the work and had forty percent interest in the project as did the Union Pacific Railroad Company. W. S. Moore Company had a twenty percent interest.[17]

Construction, exploration and development work continued in 1969. The mill was reportedly placed into operation mid-year, but no production was reported. The Natural Resources Division of the Union Pacific Railroad Company assumed management from the Cleveland-Cliffs Iron Company on June 1, 1969.[18]

Tom Bond III joined the exploration effort at Summitville in the spring of 1969 and was on loan for six months from Union Pacific Railroad's exploration division to perform underground geologic evaluation. He stated that the project had several goals at that time: 1) Develop a high-grade copper-silver mine based on

Covellite and Gold – Reynolds Tunnel
Courtesy of V. W. "Bill" Ellithorpe

the unmined but previously drilled Missionary deposit; 2) Mine some of the high-grade pods left in the Reynolds workings. One pod of copper ore in the back of a drift was at least twenty-five feet long, a foot wide and solid covellite; 3) When the project had been established, drill some deep holes along the edge of the Summitville Caldera to explore the possibility of a porphyry copper deposit at considerable depth; and 4) In the future modify the mill for mining the low-grade gold ore above the Reynolds Tunnel.[19]

Summitville is a noted locality for the copper mineral covellite, CuS or copper sulfide. The Reynolds workings were mined in the early 1970s and many covellite specimens were produced that ended up in mineral collections worldwide. The best covellite crystals are well-formed deep-blue hexagonal plates up to ¾ inches across.[20]

Unfortunately all of the exploration efforts to define mineable copper reserves at Summitville failed. When the copper ore body was accessed by drifts driven into it from the shaft, it was found that the high-grade copper ore was very erratic and not suitable for underground mining; and a sufficient grade of ore could not be maintained for an economical operation. A decision was then made in late 1969 by Union Pacific Railroad and Cleveland-Cliffs to abandon the project. However, at that point, W. S. Moore formed a joint venture with Quad construction, Frontier Resources and Polaris Resources to continue work on the copper mill and mine.[21]

High-grade copper ore containing silver and gold was mined and stockpiled in 1970 for milling when the mill was completed. The estimated cost of the mill was $500,000.[22]

The mill was completed mid-1971 and put into operation. Production continued to increase and amounted to 215,000 pounds of copper in 1971.[23] The Summitville mine and mill stopped all operations in 1972. Recorded production for the year was 205 troy ounces of gold, 3,265 troy ounces of silver and 202,000 pounds of copper. Declining ore reserves caused the shutdown.[24]

Tom Bond III told of his memories of Summitville[25]:

When I first went to Summitville in May 1969, the old gold mill was nothing but a rotting pile of old timber. The main building was a two-story frame structure. The ground floor had a warehouse at one end. It became the core shack, a shower and dry for the staff, two offices and a large engineering and geology office across one end. This office had a beautiful map-model of the workings above the Reynolds Tunnel drawn on glass plates. The second floor had a kitchen, a dining room and a dozen or so bedrooms. Cleveland-Cliffs had brought a cook and her husband down from Michigan. Jesse was an excellent cook and could bake good cakes at an elevation of 11,300 feet. She earned the trust of a family of pine martins to the point where they would take food from her hand. Their trust was betrayed as her husband later trapped the martins for their pelts. At one end of the old warehouse were two large cans of cyanide alongside two-five-gallon carboys of sulfuric acid. I always thought if we ever had a fire I would run upwind as far and fast as possible. This building did indeed burn at some later date.

There were a number of other old buildings in various states of repair. For an isolated property, Summitville was unique in having a high-pressure gas line through the property. One day in October, the purchasing agent went running out of the office to stop a snowplow operator from banging on the 800 pound per square inch gas line.

Exploration

After the end of the Missionary deposit project in 1972, Bill Bird and Associates of Vancouver, British Columbia, interested American Smelting & Refining Company (ASARCO) in drilling some deep holes along the edge of the Summitville Caldera to explore the possibility of a porphyry copper deposit at considerable depth. This drilling had been in Union Pacific Railroad's long-range plan.[26]

In 1973, several mineral exploration companies were shown Reynolds' Summitville property by Joe Mathews, a Texas oilman who was acting as a land broker for the owner, Reynolds Mining Company, and ASARCO was awarded the lease.[27]

Reynolds-Morse Corporation had been dissolved about 1956 for tax reasons when selling the Summitville property to General Minerals Company had been a distinct possibility. A family limited partnership, the Reynolds Mining Company, was formed in 1965 to manage all the properties of the Reynolds estate.[28]

ASARCO was interested in both the copper and gold potential of Summitville. Under the direction of chief geologist C. E. Beverly, two holes were drilled to test the theory of a porphyry copper deposit at depth. One hole was 3,000 feet deep and the other 4,700 feet deep. Unfortunately copper values necessary to support a mine were not found and the deep exploration for copper was abandoned. ASARCO also drilled about 400 shallow holes and 12 deeper holes to evaluate the potential of open-pit gold mining and, not satisfied with the results, dropped their lease. Even though ASARCO decided not to pursue gold mining at Summitville, the company identified a significant shallow low-grade gold deposit.[29]

In late afternoon of October 3, 1975, Bob Ellithorpe, an employee of ASARCO, happened to look down while operating a bulldozer. He noticed a large unusually colored rock along the road he was building. Some time later he went back to inspect it and found himself looking at more gold in that rock than he had ever dreamed of seeing. The story of the rock he found, named the Summitville Gold Boulder, will be told later in this chapter.[30]

The Reynolds Mining Company then gave a lease on the shallow low-grade deposit located by ASARCO to C. E. Beverly, who was ASARCO's chief geologist; Bill Bird, the geologist who initially interested ASARCO; and a Mr. Buqui. These three individuals, who were called the "Three Bees," promoted Summitville's open-pit gold mining potential. Anaconda Minerals Company was interested in investigating several mining properties in southwestern Colorado, including Summitville. In July 1979 the shallow lease was assigned to Anaconda and an extensive exploration program was conducted over a five-year period consisting of 389 drill holes totaling 133,000 feet. A sample preparation laboratory was built north of Monte Vista, several metallurgical investigations on gold recovery were made, and environmental studies for a mine permit were initiated.[31]

In the late 1970s or early 1980s, V. W. "Bill" Ellithorpe and his brother Bob had a three year lease on a small section of ground about 1,000 yards north of the Pickens' Cut and sank a shaft to a depth of fifty feet on the lease. The shaft was named the Beverly Shaft in honor of C. E. Beverly, ASARCO's geologist and a good friend of the Ellithorpes. A shipment of twenty tons of ore was made to the Leadville smelter that ran one troy ounce of gold per ton. This shipment was most likely the last ore mined by underground methods in the Summitville district. When the Ellithorpe's lease ran out, Anaconda Minerals Company took it over.[32]

John R. King, Anaconda's district geologist, discussed the Summitville operations at a meeting with the Alamosa County Chamber of Commerce in June 1981.[33] Anaconda began work in 1980 at Summitville on May 15, with about thirty drillers, contractors, samplers, and geologists. Another sixty people worked in the sample preparation laboratory. The work continued through September and into October and November. King stated that Summitville's very low-grade deposit would require an open pit operation with side canyons used as waste dumps. The dumps would be covered over and reclaimed. He guessed that the

The Beverly Shaft
Courtesy of W. V. "Bill" Ellithorpe

amount mined daily would be 1,000 to 2,000 tons, assuming that there would be a mine.

Anaconda could not come up with an economical and viable mine plan. After spending four years and more than $6 million the company dropped its lease in March 1984.[34]

The Ellithorpe brothers, V. W. "Bill" and Robert M., purchased about 250 acres of Summitville mining claims from their uncle Ralph C. Ellithorpe's wife in 1973. The largest claim in the group was the Bowen Placer, Mineral Survey No. 267, located by Thomas M. Bowen and others on November 11, 1879. The Ellithorpes leased their claims to ASARCO until the ASARCO leases were dropped. After lengthy negotiations, the property was sold to Anaconda Minerals Company for $2.2 million.[35]

The Summitville Gold Boulder[36]

After Bob Ellithorpe inspected the large unusually colored rock along the road he was building and found himself looking at more gold in the rock than he had ever dreamed of seeing, he approached his friend C. E. "Chuck" Beverly, ASARCO's chief geologist at Summitville, and asked him if he would like to see the gold-filled rock. Beverly certainly wanted to see the rock and agreed to give Bob half of the gold for finding it. The two drove to the site of the rock, partly hidden by a three-foot pine tree growing along one side and an eight-inch pine growing on top of the rock. Even so, the gold streaks in the rock were easy to see. The Dexter Adit was about 100 feet to the left of the rock. Its location was at the end of a snowslide area that began at the top of the Del Norte Claim where Jack Pickens' Cut was.

The Summitville Golden Boulder in its Original Location
*Bob Ellithorpe is on the left and C. E. "Chuck" Beverly is on the right
Courtesy of V. W. "Bill" Ellithorpe*

Beverly examined the rock and agreed that the streaks were indeed gold, more than he had ever seen in a small boulder. He told Ellithorpe that he could see why he wanted half the gold and that there was plenty for everyone. By then the sun had set and it was getting dark, so the two men decided to leave the rock in place so they could document it and its location in the morning with photographs. The next morning two men lifted the rock and placed it in a metal box and into a pickup. Then the rock was taken to the boarding house where it was washed with soapy water to remove mud and lichens. Washing the rock also removed enough fine gold to fill a vial with ¼ inches of gold crystals.

Beverly described the rock in his official report as follows:

The flat boulder, 18 inches by approximately 12 inches in diameter and weighing 141.5 pounds, is intrusive breccia consisting of silicified vuggy quartz latite fragments cemented with a matrix of very fine-grained crystalline quartz, barite and gold. The gold appears to wrap around most of the fragments in a spectacular arrangement. The largest gold vein measures 12 inches by 0.6 inches and appears to cut entirely through the breccia mass. At this stage, the gold appears to be directly related to the matrix and a primary crystallization feature. At least one 1/8 inch gold crystal is present along the vein.

Shortly after discovery of the gold-bearing rock, Beverly called his boss, Stephen Von Fay, at the ASARCO office in Denver to tell him of the find and his agreement with Bob Ellithorpe to give him half the gold's value as a finder's fee. Within the week, Von Fay met with Bill Ellithorpe to negotiate the finder's fee. The rock was appraised and its value set at about $50,000, given the fact that the rock contained 350 troy ounces of gold, or about twenty-four pounds. ASARCO offered him 39.2 percent of the gross bullion value of the gold, or $21,000, and he accepted.

Ellithorpe divided the finder's fee equally between his brother, father and himself. Unfortunately, Bill's father died less than a month after the discovery and did not live long enough to see his share.

ASARCO kept the discovery a secret for a year and then made a decision, in concurrence with Bob Ellithorpe and the Reynolds Mining Company, to donate the Summitville Gold

Boulder to the Denver Museum of Natural History, where it is now on display.

The following photograph shows Harry and Bob Ellithorpe, V. W. "Bill" Ellithorpe's father and brother, admiring the Summitville Gold Boulder at the boarding house after it had been cleaned. Harry, who was in his eighties and dying of throat cancer, traveled from Colorado Springs to Summitville to see the rock his son had found.

Courtesy of V. W. "Bill" Ellithorpe

Harry worked for Jack Pickens and ran a prospect crew from the Colorado School of Mines during the time A. O. Smith operated Summitville. Bob also worked for A. O. Smith before World War II. Bill's uncle, Ralph, was the administrator for the Thomas Bowen estate and wrote *Poker, Politics and Gold*, published by the Denver Westerners, Inc. in their 1971 *Brand Book*. He also was District Court Reporter in Del Norte. The book is about Thomas M. Bowen and the history of Summitville and is referenced many times in this book.

CHAPTER 6
GALACTIC RESOURCES, INC.
1984-1992

As previously noted, the rebirth of Summitville's mining was primarily due to the Gold Reserve Act of 1934, when the government began purchasing gold at $35 per troy ounce instead of at the previous price of $20.67. By 1961, it became apparent that the $35 per troy ounce fixed gold price and rising inflation had essentially eliminated mining gold in the United States and elsewhere in the world. A pool of U. S. and European banks agreed to manipulate the market to prevent further currency devaluation against the increased gold demand not being met.

On March 17, 1968, economic circumstances caused a collapse of the gold pool and a two-tiered pricing scheme was established whereby gold was still used to settle international accounts at $35 per troy ounce, but the price of gold on the private market was allowed to fluctuate. The two-tiered price system was abandoned in 1975 and the price of gold was left to find its free market level. The free-market price for gold had risen to $423.01 per troy ounce in 1983, setting the stage for the next mining activity at Summitville.

Production for the district from 1870 through 1983 was 258,074 troy ounces of gold and 432,886 troy ounces of silver. There is no official record of gold and silver production from 1984 through 1992. However, one unofficial source lists 294,365 troy ounces of gold and 319,814 troy ounces of silver for the period or fifty-three percent of the district's total production of gold and forty-two percent of its total production of silver.

As the smaller high-grade deposits such as that at Summitville were depleted in the mid-twentieth century, the mining industry began mining large low-grade deposits primarily by open pit methods. These methods were first developed to mine iron and copper in the United States. This was made possible through intensive mechanization and the use of technology to reduce labor costs. One unfortunate side effect of such large-scale mining has been the impact on the environment – large pits in the earth and large piles of waste rock and tailings.

Open-pit mining methods were successfully used by AMAX, Inc. at its molybdenum mine at Climax, north of Leadville, Colorado. This mine, at an elevation of 11,600 feet, has similar topographic and weather characteristics as the Summitville area. The Anaconda Minerals Company's exploration at Summitville in the early 1980s had defined a low-grade gold and silver ore body that would require open pit mining to be economical. As stated in Chapter Five, Anaconda did not develop an economical and viable mine plan and dropped their lease in March 1984.

Robert Friedland organized a new company, Galactic Resources, Limited, of Vancouver, British Columbia, Canada, for mining projects. A subsidiary, Galactic Resources, Inc., was formed in the United States for the same purpose. Galactic Resources, Inc. obtained a lease on the Reynolds Mining Company's Summitville property in April 1984. The company announced that the low-grade ore body at Summitville contained an estimated million troy ounces of gold averaging 0.045 troy ounces of gold per ton, and they proposed using a heap leach method of recovery for surface mined ore[1].

Heap leaching is a technique that has been applied to the recovery of metals such as copper or gold and silver from low-grade ores. The ore is placed on an impervious plastic membrane installed over a prepared soil surface sloping to a low point beneath the leach pad. A dilute solution of sulfuric acid in the case of copper or cyanide for precious metals is then sprayed on the upper surface of the ore and allowed to percolate downward through the heap dissolving the metal values and then flowing to a collection sump at the low point beneath the pad. The solution with the dissolved metal is drained by gravity to an external pond and is then pumped to a facility where the metal is recovered and the solution returned to the leach pad where the leaching cycle is repeated. This procedure keeps the hydraulic head on the pad liner low, only a few feet. As will be described later, the heap leach pad at Summitville was actually an enclosed basin because no relatively flat land for a standard pad was present at the Summitville site.

Galactic believed that, by using open-pit mining and heap leach processing, the Summitville low-grade ore could be profitably mined. Galactic Resources, Inc. organized a subsidiary, the Summitville Consolidated Mining Company, Inc., for mining operations at Summitville. This company purchased Anaconda's data and, during the summer of 1984, completed the exploration drilling required to accurately define the ore reserves.[2]

The Summitville Consolidated Mining Company, Inc. entered into a contract with Bechtel Civil and Minerals Inc. of San Francisco, California in 1984 to develop plans for a mine and leaching operation. The operation would be capable of producing 120,000 troy ounces of gold and 50,000 troy ounces of silver per year for a minimum of five years from the ore deposit that had proven reserves of 18 million tons of ore.[3]

Galactic Resources, Inc. obtained a limited impact permit from the Colorado Mined Land Reclamation Division of the Department of Natural Resources authorizing no more than ten acres of disturbance. This permit was required for the construction of four test heaps to determine the feasibility of heap-leaching technology at Summitville. Approximately 16,600 tons of ore were processed in the pilot test program in the summer of 1984.[4] Heap-leaching tests recovered about 1,000 ounces of gold and indicated that heap-leaching was economically viable.[5]

On August 25, 1984, the Mined Land Reclamation Division of the Colorado Department of Natural Resources approved a permit application for full-scale mine development.[6] This occurred less than five months after Galactic Resources, Inc. secured a lease on the Summitville property. State regulators gave Galactic the benefit of many doubts and approved the permit as fast as – maybe faster than – the law allowed.[7] It is amazing that few, if any, baseline studies to determine the environmental criteria in the Summitville area, such as weather conditions and existing water quality that was affected both by natural pollution and earlier mining, were required by the state or were conducted by Galactic or its contractors.

Open-Pit Mining and Heap Leaching

Economies of scale for mining at Summitville changed dramatically with the open-pit proposed by Galactic Resources, Inc. (Refer to the Prologue for a map showing the pit limits.) Summitville had produced 282,400 tons of ore in the period 1935 through 1942 by underground mining methods, or an average of 35,300 tons per year. The average ore grade was 0.375 troy ounces of gold.[8] Summitville Consolidated Mining Company, Inc.'s daily mining rate of waste rock or overburden (defined as containing less than 0.01 troy ounces of gold per ton) and ore would average 35,000 tons per day during the six-month mining periods each year of operation. Each day the company would mine nearly as much rock as was mined by underground mining methods in the average year for the period 1935 through 1942. The average ore grade for the same underground mining period, 0.375 troy ounces of gold per ton, was 8.33 times greater than the grade of ore, 0.045 troy ounces of gold per ton, mined from the open pit. Productivity during the underground mining period was in the range of one ton of ore mined per man-shift as compared to Summitville Consolidated Mining Company, Inc. productivity of about 500 tons per man-shift.[9]

The use of a dilute alkaline cyanide solution to extract gold and silver from their ores was first developed in 1887. The first cyanide mill was built in New Zealand in 1889.[10] Cyanide has been widely used for gold recovery in South Africa and elsewhere since the early 1900s. Sodium cyanide (NaCN) provides the radical CN that attaches itself to gold and silver to form soluble gold or silver cyanide complexes that are then precipitated from the solution by zinc dust or adsorbed on activated carbon. The barren solution is then recycled to extract more precious metal. The solution must be maintained in an alkaline form. If the solution becomes weakly acidic, the CN radical combines with hydrogen to form hydrocyanic acid. If the solution becomes more acidic, poisonous hydrogen cyanide, a colorless gas with a faint, bitter, almond-like odor, is formed and is quickly dissipated into the atmosphere where the cyanide concentration becomes minimal.

According to the Agency for Toxic Substances & Disease Registry, exposure to high levels of cyanide compounds harms the brain and heart and may cause coma and death. Hydrogen cyanide gas was used in years past in some states to execute those condemned to death by the courts. Exposure to lower cyanide levels may result in breathing difficulties, heart pains, and vomiting. Cyanide is found in a number of foods and plants, including tapioca, almonds, lima beans, soy beans, and spinach. Cyanide compounds are used in electroplating, metallurgy and mining, organic chemical production, photography, and the manufacture of plastics.

As described in Chapter 3, A. E. Reynolds' attempt to use a cyanide process to extract gold in 1902 was not successful. Cyanide was used to treat Summitville flotation tailings in the 1930s.

Newmont Mining Corporation first employed heap leaching with cyanide solution to recover gold at the Carlin Mine near Elko, Nevada in the 1960s. The method quickly spread to other mines in Nevada.

The first outdoor heap-leaching project in Colorado using cyanide recovered gold in existing mine dumps and mill tailings took place in the Cripple Creek mining district in 1976. The Cripple Creek & Victor Gold Mining Company began open-pit mining and heap leaching at the Portland Mine in 1988. The use of open-pit mining and cyanide heap leaching has been used at Cripple Creek since then, to this day successfully and safely. However, conditions at Cripple Creek are much different than at Summitville. Evaporation greatly exceeds precipitation at Cripple Creek, and water from the underground mines is slightly basic instead of being acidic like that at Summitville.

Galactic's permit required that the open-pit mine and heap leach pads were to have "zero" discharge of waste water from their operation. In the original design an incorrect assumption was made that evaporation losses would be greater than the combined effects of precipitation and makeup water additions.[11] This was not to be the case. A base line study of weather conditions at Summitville would have clearly shown that precipitation far exceeded evaporation, and that the original design of uncovered leach pads with a resulting "zero" discharge was not possible.

Construction of the mine and plant facilities commenced in late 1984, but was abruptly stopped because of the lack of finances and the fact that the price of gold had dropped from $423.01 in 1983 to $360.81 per troy ounce. By mid-1985 additional financing was secured and construction re-started. Most of the construction was done during the winter of 1985-86, with a labor force of over 400 people bused from the nearby town of South Fork. No one lived in Summitville. Construction of the heap leach system continued during the winter in spite of the risks and difficulties of winter construction at Summitville. Snow avalanches in March and April caused significant damages to the soil geo-membrane liner and delayed completion of construction.[12]

Galactic's Mining and Milling Operations

Galactic's Summitville mining and milling operations were described by Stanley H. Dayton in an article in the August 1986 *Engineering and Mining Journal* entitled "Galactic pumps new life into Summitville:"

Old gold districts may fade into the background but never seem to die away. Such is the case of the acidic volcanics near Summitville, Colo., where Canada's Galactic Resources Ltd. became a new entry in the North American gold rush last May with a $46 million heap leaching project on low grade ore.

Galactic aims at the recovery of 120,000 troy ounces of gold and 60,000 troy ounces of silver during 1986 and a steady-state gold output of approximately 100,000 troy ounces (plus by-product silver) thereafter at a predicted cash operating cost of $175 per troy ounce.

Perched near the 12,600-foot summit of South Mountain in Colorado's San Juan Range, Galactic has identified ore reserves of 25.3 million tons grading 0.042 ounces of gold per ton. Of that

The Open Pit with the Plant in the Background –
August 3, 1988

total, 16.2 million tons is open pittable at a cutoff of 0.01 ounces per ton – an amount sufficient to cover a six-year seasonal mining plan at an overall stripping ratio of 1.67 tons of waste to 1 ton of ore.

Through its wholly-owned operating arm, Summitville Consolidated Mining Company, Inc., Galactic entered producer ranks, utilizing the services of a stripping and mining contractor, Industrial Constructors Corporation, a subsidiary of Washington Corporation based in Missoula, Montana. The physical plant at Summitville consists of:

1. An open pit near the crest of South Mountain to be benched between the 11,400 and 12,250-foot elevations, an altitude that yields downhill truck haulage during most of the six-year mining plan.

2. A 28,800 ton per day primary and secondary crushing and screening plant.

3. Twin 4,000-foot conveyors systems – one delivering crushed silica ore to a heap leach truck load-out bin and the other transporting clay ores to a three-belt agglomerator where they are lightly bound using cement and water additions prior to being trucked to the leach heaps.

4. A 25 acre heap leach site, expandable to 106 acres, that features a buried "insitu" pregnant solution reservoir trapped behind a plastic-lined, earth fill dam containing the leach heaps; the reservoir is tapped via submersible pumps in perforated 12-foot diameter steel-cased wells embedded in the ore heaps.

5. A 3,000 gallon per minute, six-stage counter current carbon adsorption module, believed to be the largest flow-rate in the world.

6. Twin pressure-stripper vessels (each capable of desorbing gold from 3-ton batches of loaded carbon) along with acid washing and carbon reactivation facilities.

7. A modified Merrill-Crowe gold precipitator (using zinc dust and two plate and frame filter presses) to recover precious metal slimes from the enriched stripper solution.

8. A tilting crucible refining furnace for the recovery of dore' bullion from oven-dried precipitates.

Secondary Crusher and Screening Plant– July 1986

9. *A power plant consisting of six Caterpillar natural gas fired generators equipped with an exhaust manifold heat recovery system; reclaimed Btu's are used for preheating leach solutions, gaining seasonal extensions for the gold recovery program.*

Ore testing, plant design and construction engineering were supervised by Bechtel Civil and Minerals, Inc. under a $21 million contract containing construction scheduling, operating cost and plant performance guarantees. Bechtel subcontracted plant erection to The Industrial Company of Steamboat Springs, Colorado.

History of Galactic's Summitville Operations

Galactic's Summitville project did not proceed as planned but ended in its abandonment and bankruptcy for Galactic Resources, Ltd. and its subsidiaries.

Most but not all of the following information on Summitville operations was taken from a Knight Piesold and Company report prepared for the Summitville Study Group in 1993.[13] A group of industry and environmental representatives jointly funded a technical and environmental study of the Summitville mine made by Knight Piesold & Company, a Denver-based consulting group of engineers and environmental scientists. The study was made to get answers to concerns over the leakage of acid, cyanide and heavy metals. The goal of the study was to develop an objective base line for the Summitville site and to present facts. The study was conducted independently from the Environmental Protection Agency's work.[14] An unstated but most important objective of this study was to counteract overblown media reporting and provide information that the mining industry could use to counteract arguments based on Summitville issues that would be raised in permitting activities elsewhere.

Open pit mining started in May of 1986 after the initial phase of the heap leach pad, actually an enclosed basin, was constructed. The heap leach basin, located in the Cropsy Creek drainage, affected about fifty acres. It was constructed in phases until early 1988. The heap leach system was located between two dikes on the upstream and downstream ends of the Cropsy Creek

Basin. The downstream dike was the larger of the two as the basin sloped downward towards it. The basin between the two dikes and the inside faces of the dikes were lined with a composite soil/geo-membrane liner covered by an eighteen-inch layer of crushed, screened ore to protect the liner system from being torn when the first level of coarse ore was loaded onto the heap leach.

A French drain system was constructed beneath the basin liner system to provide drainage for flows, such as springs, that might occur beneath the basin liner. The cyanide solution, sprayed over the top of the leach heap, percolated down through the crushed ore to be collected in two twelve-foot diameter vertical sumps located at the low point of the basin. Hydraulic head on the liner system would be kept low because of continuous de-watering of the pad liner by the recovery pumps located in the bottom of the sumps.

Unfortunately, cost cutting measures were taken at the expense of accepted leach pad construction techniques during the actual wintertime construction. An eyewitness remarked that the crushed ore was, in some cases, placed on the geo-membrane without the designed eighteen-inch layer of fine material placed

Placing Crushed Ore on the Heap Leach Pad – July 1986

over the membrane to protect it. This resulted in tears in the geo-membrane. Also the outer slopes of the heap above the basin were made steeper than a stable slope for the crushed ore in order to maximize the volume of ore placed in the heap over the permitted pad area. When the steep slopes were saturated with cyanide solution and snow melt, they failed, and the ore above a stable slope slid downward and caused failures in the geo-membrane.

Application of leach solution began June 5, 1986 and, on June 10, cyanide solution was detected in the leak detection system beneath the liner, only five days later. As a result, Summitville Consolidated Mining Company installed a permanent french drain sump and pump back system to return the leaking cyanide solution to the leach pad or a treatment plant. Between June and October 1987 nine cyanide spills occurred from this system resulting in the discharge of about 85,000 gallons of dilute cyanide solution into Cropsy Creek.

Heap Leach System with Plant and Mine in the Background –
September 11, 1993
Courtesy of Intrasearch, Inc.

As previously mentioned, the original design of the heap leach system assumed that evaporation losses of water at Summitville would exceed precipitation and the addition of makeup water to the system. This, of course, was not correct and was a fatal flaw to the system. As stated in the Prologue, precipitation greatly exceeds evaporation at Summitville. A rumor denied by state officials, alleged that the precipitation evaporation data for the original heap leach design was from Alamosa, which is located in the arid San Luis Valley. Later analyses of the precipitation/evaporation balance suggested removal of snow from the heap leach pad, or shaping it to provide snow melt runoff, and covering it with geo-membrane to prevent inflow of the snow melt into the pad. This was impractical and was not done.

Galactic's permit required "zero" discharge of contaminated water and, therefore, the only immediate solution was to store the excess contaminated water in the leach pad basin. This raised the water level in the heap leach basin to about 100 feet above the low point and created increased hydraulic pressure on the liner leaks, permitting more escaping solution. Fresh water springs beneath the liner increased the leakage into a larger volume of more dilute, but still contaminated, water.

By late 1987, Summitville Consolidated Mines, Inc. was aware that water from the snow melt was fast accumulating in the heap leach basin, and on February 2, 1988 the company applied for a permit to discharge treated water from the heap leach basin. Discharge would be in accordance with the Colorado Pollutant Discharge System, under the National Pollutant Discharge Elimination System administered by the Environmental Protection Agency. It was reported that if Summitville experienced a normal winter precipitation, the heap leach solution would overtop the downstream dike spillway by December of 1989, sooner if a wetter than normal winter occurred.

The company applied for a discharge permit to allow the treatment and release of the excess process solution. The Water Quality Control Division of the Colorado Department of Health approved the permit in May 1989, and the Mined Land Reclamation Division of the Colorado Department of Natural Resources approved plans for the plant's installation.

The water treatment plant was assembled in the mill building that had been constructed in 1968 by the W. S. Moore – Cleveland Cliffs – Union Pacific Railroad joint venture. The plant was designed to treat 500,000 gallons of contaminated water per day from the French drain sumps. These sumps collected cyanide solution leaking from the leach heap basin. The treated water was then to be released into Wightman Fork. This would eliminate pumping this water back into the heap and would allow the water level in the heap to decrease, thus reducing the volume of cyanide solution leaking through the liner into the French drain system. The plant was designed to precipitate metals from solution by adding lime and to destroy cyanide by treating the solution with chlorine. A polishing step was included to remove very low levels of metal ions remaining after the lime treatment, and an aeration step was included to remove residual chlorine from solution.

The plant was able to meet all the required effluent limitations except for silver. Reportedly, the state's silver limitation was less than one part per billion and was set to protect brook trout and other species in waters downstream. Even though an independent laboratory tested the effluent for silver and came up with no measurable silver using an industry-accepted method of analysis, the state refused to permit discharge of the effluent directly into Wightman Fork.

The Mined Land Reclamation Division then gave their approval for land application of the excess treated water as a method of polishing and disposal rather than discharge to the stream. In July 1989, land application commenced on a five-acre site. In July 1990, the Water Quality Control Division found that the land application system was malfunctioning and the contaminated discharge was flowing directly into Wightman Fork. Land application was discontinued on October 30, 1991.

Mining and pad loading was stopped in October of 1991. Ore processing ceased the spring of 1992. By the fall of 1992, site grading of the test heap-leach pad and its immediate area and placement of topsoil thereon had been completed.

Galactic Resources, Ltd. sold nearly all of its mining assets to cover reclamation costs at Summitville. In December 1991 the company agreed to sell its forty-eight percent interest in the

Ridgeway Mine in South Carolina to the Kennecott Corporation, its fifty percent stake in the Ivanhoe Mine in Nevada, and its properties in California.

The Summitville Consolidated Mining Company dropped its lease on the Reynolds Mining Company's Summitville property and filed for bankruptcy under Chapter 7 of the U.S. bankruptcy laws in early December of 1992. The company announced that it would stop all site operations at Summitville on December 15, 1992, thus ending mining at Summitville that stretched back to the discovery of gold in 1870.

Highland Mary Ore Sorting Room and Bin - July 1986

One of the last remaining structures from early-day underground mining at Summitville was demolished to make way for the Galactic open pit mine in the summer of 1986. This structure, an ore sorting room and ore bin where the ore was stored until it could be hauled to the mill by truck, was connected to the Highland Mary Mine by a snow tunnel covering the tracks from the mine located about 300 feet from the Dexter Tunnel. The structure was built in the 1930s. Weathered wood from the structure was salvaged and used to make antique looking items such as picture frames.

On December 4, 1992, the Colorado Department of Health requested an emergency response action from the Environmental Protection Agency to maintain the Summitville site because the cyanide solution in the heap-leach basin was within a few feet of overtopping the downstream dike. Galactic Resources, Limited filed for bankruptcy in Canada on January 26, 1993. The Environmental Protection Agency granted itself a variance to release the excess solution to save the dam, something that the Water Quality Control Division of the Colorado Department of Health had refused when requested by the Summitville Consolidated Mining Company. The Environmental Protection Agency's fast response and efforts stopped the overtopping of the heap-leach basin's downstream dike, which could have released a mixture of contaminated water and crushed ore into Wightman Fork with potentially disastrous effects on the Alamosa and Rio Grande River watersheds.

The Summitville problems focused national attention on the environmental effects of modern mineral resource development – primarily large-scale open-pit mining operations. At least one Colorado county government banned the use of cyanide in mining operations as a result of Summitville.

A baseline study of the Alamosa River and its tributaries (Iron, Alum, Bitter and Burnt Creek and Wightman Fork) prior to Galactic's mining operation would have shown that the Alamosa was devoid of a fish population from its confluence with Iron Creek downstream to its confluence with non-polluted tributaries from the south out of the area of acid/sulfate alteration as described in the Prologue. Stopping the discharge of treated water from the Galactic plant did not save non-existent brook trout.

The news media covered Summitville and its environmental problems – real or imagined – intensely. Papers as far away as the *New York Times* carried stories of the "disaster." One Denver newspaper article in 1991 stated that "Deadly cyanide-laced water, from a large gold mine near Wolf Creek Pass has killed all aquatic life in seventeen miles of the Alamosa River and the Terrace Reservoir say state and federal officials." Not at all true, but quite likely believed by most of the paper's readers.

It is true that the original Galactic heap-leach pad design was fatally flawed; that short cuts in the construction of the heap leach system and improper loading caused serious leakage problems of cyanide solution; and the proper baseline studies were not required or made prior to permitting the project. Quite likely the Colorado state legislature's cutting the Mined Land Reclamation Department's budget at that time had a negative effect on the department's ability to do its job. It is most unfortunate that the regulators and media assumed that man (the mining industry) was responsible for all of the pollution and did not accept the fact that the Alamosa River has been continuously polluted by Mother Nature, probably dating back more than 10,000 years prior to any mining at Summitville.

Imagine how different the end of the Summitville story might have been if Galactic had been allowed to discharge the treated water as was done by the Environmental Protection Agency when they took over Summitville!

Aerial Photograph of Summitville Mine by Intrasearch taken
October 4, 1991
Colorado Geological Survey Special Publication 38, *Proceedings: Summitville Forum*

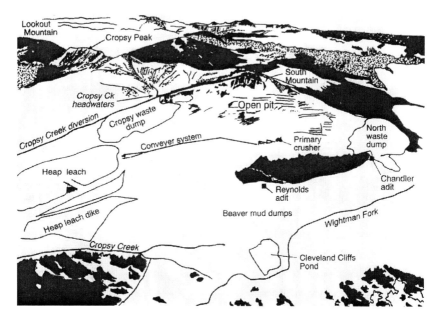

Line Drawing of Summitville Mine Photograph by Richard Walker
Colorado Geological Survey Special Publication 38, *Proceedings: Summitville Forum*

Production values from 1870 through 1923 are from Henderson, Charles W., *Mining in Colorado*, U. S. Geological Survey Professional paper No. 138. Henderson's gold values are given in dollars. These have been converted to troy ounces by dividing annual dollar values by the average gold price for the specific year as given in *Gold Statistics*, U. S. Geological Survey. Production values from 1924 through 1985 are from *Mineral Resources of the U. S.* and the *Colorado Bureau of Mines Annual Reports*. There are no official production reports from 1986 through 1992. An unofficial source of information is quoted.

PRODUCTION
Gold, Silver, Copper and Lead Production at Summitville
1870 – 1992

Year	Gold Troy Ounces	Silver Troy Ounces	Copper Pounds	Lead Pounds
1870	Not Recorded	---	---	---
1873	96.76	---	---	---
1874	241.90	---	---	---
1875	13,161.30	7,734	---	---
1876	5,861.06	7,734	---	---
1877	9,450.27	7,734	---	---
1878	4,976.58	7,734	---	---
1879	1,378.81	7,734	---	---
1880	290.28	---	---	---
1881	14,029.00	7,734	---	---
1882	10,159.65	15,469	---	---
1883	8,708.27	7,734	---	---
1884	6,289.31	10,828	---	---
1885	6,289.31	9,800	---	---
1886	7,221.38	8,817	---	---
1887	5,920.66	7,992	---	---
1888	786.65	2,923	---	---
1889	1,730.04	3,757	---	---
1890	1,244.12	1,287	---	---
1891	1,867.05	7,752	---	---
1892	700.87	12,526	---	---
1893	---	796	---	---
1894	813.55	1,260	---	---
1895	764.15	3,359	---	---
1896	90.47	1,353	1,369	451
1897	1,092.99	8,168	627	12,006
1898	179.97	1,568	9,794	2,393
1899	928.98	2,718	336	1,635
1900	5,682.63	3,075	8,599	26,260
1901	1,735.74	6,926	65,603	677
1902	753.01	3,171	1,260	166
1903	683.16	3,410	5,098	---
1904	212.06	2,281	650	---
1905	214.57	1,055	123	---
1906	453.73	152	---	---

Year	Gold Troy Ounce	Silver Troy Ounces	Copper Pounds	Lead Pounds
1907	---	---	---	---
1908	40.34	---	---	---
1909	---	---	---	---
1910	69.06	61	87	250
1911	---	---	---	---
1912	292.98	896	29,673	313
1913	12.85	109	568	---
1914	24.99	16	---	---
1915	781.21	325	---	---
1916	---	---	---	---
1917	1.23	52	---	1,930
1918	---	---	---	---
1919	---	---	---	---
1920	---	---	---	---
1921	---	---	---	---
1922	---	---	---	---
1923	80.40	161	218	929
1924	172.12	109	---	1,600
1925	121.80	477	---	4,500
1926	5,118.02	88	---	---
1927	6,459.51	268	---	---
1928	11,879.88	607	---	---
1929	1,634.21	6,058	5,392	55,237
1930	415.54	239	---	1,500
1931	50.94	79	---	---
1932	9.00	7	---	---
1933	181.81	28	---	200
1934	1,201.06	2,393	6,000	---
1935	8,119.00	12,423	45,000	---
1936	12,991.14	25,271	70,000	---
1937	15,369.40	34,053	29,000	1,200
1938	19,768.60	50,855	10,000	---
1939	14,445.00	53,460	---	---
1940	12,037.00	37,215	130,000	---
1941	16,979.00	14,019	8,000	---
1942	5,499.00	7,186	93,000	800
1943	3,287.00	1,402	17,000	---
1944	2,154.00	1,222	15,000	700
1945	560.00	675	2,400	---
1946	1,834.00	2,338	14,000	---
1947	2,129.00	2,422	18,500	2,400

Year	Gold Troy Ounce	Silver Troy Ounces	Copper Pounds	Lead Pounds
1948	---	---	---	---
1949	82.00	201	4,000	---
1950	---	---	---	---
1951	---	---	---	---
1952	---	---	---	---
1953	---	---	---	---
1954	19.00	7	---	---
1955	28.00	4	---	---
1956	---	---	---	---
1957	---	---	---	---
1958	6.00	14	10,000	---
1959	---	---	---	---
1960	---	---	---	---
1961	---	---	---	---
1962	---	---	---	---
1963	---	---	---	---
1964	---	---	---	---
1965	---	---	---	---
1966	---	---	---	---
1967	---	---	---	---
1968	---	---	---	---
1969	---	---	---	---
1970	---	---	---	---
1971	---	---	215,000	---
1972	205.00	3,265	202,000	---
1973	---	---	---	---
1974	---	---	---	---
1975	---	---	---	---
1976	---	---	---	---
1977	---	---	---	---
1978	---	---	---	---
1979	---	---	---	---
1980	---	---	---	---
1981	---	---	---	---
1982	---	---	---	---
1983	---	---	---	---
1984	---	---	---	---
1985	---	---	---	---
1986-1992	294,365.00	319,81	---	---
Totals	552,439.00	752,700	1,018,297	115,147

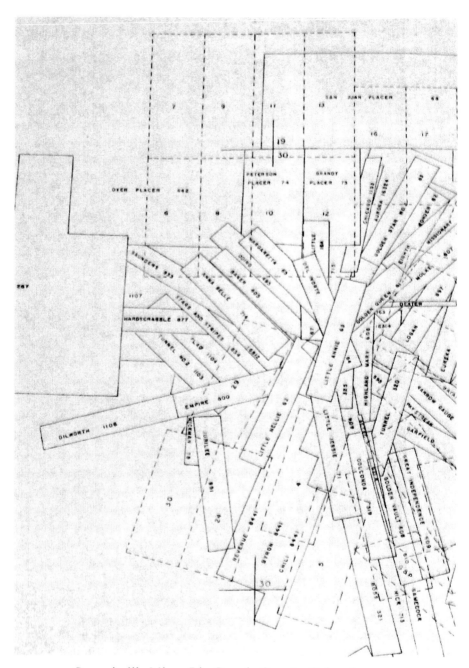

Summitville Mines Rio Grande County, Colorado
Property Map July 21 1971

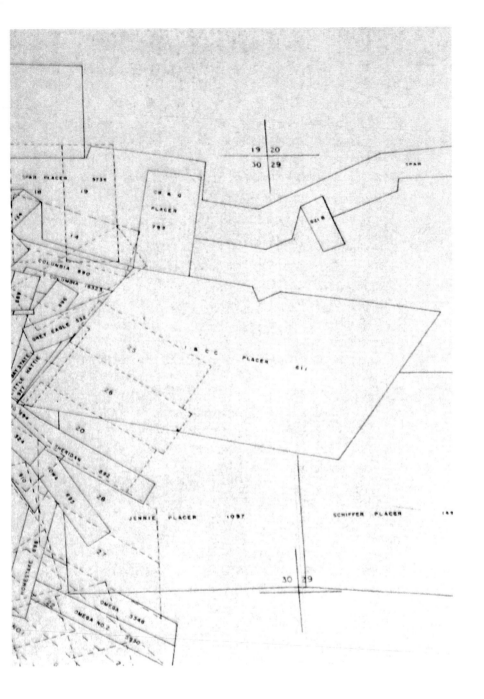

FOOTNOTES

PROLOGUE

1. Thomas A. Steven and James C. Ratte', *Geology and Ore Deposits of the Summitville District, San Juan Mountains, Colorado*, U. S. Geological Survey Professional Paper 343, 1960, p. 7.
2. *The San Luis Valley Historian*, 1982, Volume XIV, Number 4, "The Hayden Survey in the San Luis Valley, 1873-1876," pp.27-29.
3. Huston, Richard C., *A Silver Camp Called Creede*, Western Reflections Publishing Company, 2005, pp 2-5.
4. Ibid, pp. 5-6
5. Steven, Thomas A. and Lipman, Peter W., *Calderas of the San Juan Volcanic Field, Southwestern Colorado*, U.S. Geological Survey Professional Paper 958, pp. 1-2, 1976
6. Gray, J. E. and Coolbaugh, Mark F., "Geology and Geochemistry of Summitville, Colorado: An Epithermal Acid Sulfate Deposit in a Volcanic Dome," *Economic Geology*, Volume 89, p. 1907, 1994.
7. Ibid. p. 1907.
8. King, Trude V. V., Editor, *Environmental Considerations of Active and Abandoned Mine Lands: Lessons from Summitville, Colorado*, U. S. Geological Survey Bulletin 2220, pp. 8-9, 1995.
9. Letter from Charles Melbye to the author dated June 4, 2010.
10. Eckel, Edwin B., *Minerals of Colorado*, Friends of Mineralogy – Colorado, Fulcrum Publishing, p. 59, 1997.
11. Stoffgren, Roger, "Genesis of Acid-Sulfate Alteration and Gold-Copper-Silver Mineralization at Summitville, Colorado," *Economic Geology*, Volume 82, 1985, pp. 1575-1591.
12. Neubert, John, "Geology of the Upper Alamosa River Area," *Colorado Geological Survey Rock Talk*, Volume 4, Number 2, April 2001, 2001, p. 3.
13. Gray, John E. and Coolbaugh, Mark F., "Geology and Geochemistry of Summitville, Colorado: An Epithermal Acid Sulfate Deposit in a Volcanic Dome," *Economic Geology*, Volume 89, pp. 1911-1912, 1994.

14. Pendleton, James A., Posey, Harry H. and Long, Michael B., *Characterizing Summitville and Its Impacts: Setting the Scene*, Colorado Geological Survey Special Publication 38, p. 2, 1995.

15. *The San Luis Valley Historian*, 1978, Volume X, Number 3, "Snowfall of 1883-1884," p. 19.

16. Elllithorpe, Ralph C., "Poker, Politics and Gold," *Denver Westerners Brand Book* (1971), The Denver Westerners, Inc., p. 52.

17. Riddle, Jack, "Sounds Like a Lie, But Isn't," *Western Gazette*, March 12, 1961 as told by Wolle, Muriel Sibell, "This is Colorado: Special Centennial Magazine," *The Denver Post*, p. 69, June 21, 1959.

18. Nossaman, Welch, "Pioneering in the San Juan," *Colorado Magazine*, October 1957, p. 300.

19. Ibid., pp. 300-303.

20. *The San Luis Valley Historian*, Volume XXVII, Number 4, p. 42, 1995.

21. Ellithorpe, Ralph C., "Poker, Politics and Gold," *Denver Westerners Brand Book* (1971), The Denver Westerners, Inc., p. 49.

22. Colorado Mining Association, *Annual Year Book for 1938*, p. 37.

23. Arlie Stanger's memories given to the author, February 2010.

24. Letter from Tom Bond II to the author dated March 4, 2010.

CHAPTER ONE - DISCOVERY

1. Raymond, R.W., *Statistics of Mines and Mining in the States and Territories West of the Rocky Mountains for 1875*, pp.282, 326-334, 1877 as reported in Henderson, Charles W., *Mining in Colorado*, U. S. Geological Survey Professional Paper 138, 1926, pp. 201-202.

2. Letter to author from Louise Colville dated January 25, 2011.

3. Ibid.

4. Rio Grande County Clerk and Recorder, Book 3, p. 80.

5. Wolle, Muriel Sibell, *Stampede to Timberline*, 1949, pp.314-316.

6. Ellithorpe, Ralph C., "Poker, Politics and Gold," *Denver Westerners Brand Book* (1971), The Denver Westerners, Inc., p. 50.

7. Ellithorpe, Ralph C., "Poker, Politics and Gold," *Denver Westerners Brand Book* (1971), The Denver Westerners, Inc., p. 50 and pp. 54-57 and Rio Grande County Clerk and Recorder Book A, p. 87.

8. *Colorado Weekly Pueblo Chieftain*, Pueblo, Colorado, October 9, 1873

9. Rio Grande County Clerk's Record Book A, p. 87

10. Rio Grande County Clerk's Record Book A, pp. 111-113

11. Hafen, LeRoy PhD, *Colorado and Its People*, Volume II, Lewis Historical Publishing Company, p. 107.

12. Letter to author from Louise Colville dated January 25, 2011 – P. J. Peterson's biography.

13. *The San Luis Valley Historian*, 1998, Volume XXX, Number 2, "Whence the Windsor Hotel," p. 26

14. *The San Luis Valley Historian*, 1976, Volume VIII, Number 2, "San Juan Prospector clippings from Rebecca Shaw scrapbook of the 1880's and 90's," pp. 3 - 13.

15. *The San Luis Valley Historian*, 1969, Volume I, Number 2, *Dates*, p. 15.

16. *The Del Norte Prospector*, Wednesday, August 12, 1981, French tells of the early days from Arthur French's letter to Lome Wilson, his sister.

17. Letter to author from Louise Colville dated January 25, 2011.

18. *The San Luis Valley Historian*, 1976, Volume VIII, Number 2, "San Juan Prospector clippings from Rebecca Shaw scrap book of the 1880's and 90's," pp. 3–13.

19. *The San Luis Valley Historian*, 1976, Volume VIII, Number 1, "The Diary of J. Cary French, 1871, Part1," pp. 3-13 and *The San Luis Valley Historian*, 1976, Volume VIII, Number 2, "The Diary of J. Carey French, 1871, Part 2," pp. 5-17.

20. Spencer, Frank C., *The Story of the San Luis Valley*, 1975, pp. 77-78.

21. Letter to author from Louise Colville dated January 25, 2011.

CHAPTER TWO - BONANZA

1. Raymond, R. W., *Statistics of Mines and Mining in the States and Territories West of the Rocky Mountains for 1875* as reported in Henderson, Charles W., *Mining in Colorado*, U.S. Geological Survey Professional Paper 138, 1926, p. 202-203.

2. Burchard, H. C., *Report of the Director of the Mint upon the production of precious metals in the United States in 1882* as reported in Henderson, Charles W., *Mining in Colorado*, U.S. Geological Survey Professional Paper 138, 1926, p. 202-203.

3. Raymond, R. W., *Statistics of Mines and Mining in the States and Territories West of the Rocky Mountains for 1875* as reported in Henderson, Charles W., *Mining in Colorado*, U. S. Geological Survey Professional Paper 138, 1926, p. 202.

4. Espinosa, Fred, *Del Norte – Its Past and Present*, mimeograph paper, Del Norte Chamber of Commerce, 1963, p. 6.

5. Taggert, Arthur F., *Elements of Ore Dressing*, John Wiley & Sons, Inc., 1951, pp. 379-380.

6. Athearn, Robert G., *Rebel of the Rockies: A History of the Denver and Rio Grande Western Railroad*, Yale University Press, 1962, pp. 92-93 and 99.

7. Riggenbach, Emma M., *A Bridge to Yesterday*, 1982, pp. 225 and 226 and a letter to the author from Louise Colville dated March 29, 2011.

8. Burchard, H. C., *Report of the Director of the Mint upon the production of precious metals in the United States in 1881* as reported in Henderson, Charles, W., *Mining in Colorado*, U. S. Geological Survey Professional Paper 138, 1926, pp. 203-204.

9. Burchard, H. C., *Report of the Director of the Mint upon the production of precious metals in the United States in 1882* as reported in Henderson, Charles W., *Mining in Colorado*, U. S. Geological Survey Professional Paper 138, 1926, p. 204.

10. Hills, R. C., *Ore Deposits of Summit District, Rio Grande County, Colorado*, Scientific Society Proceedings, Volume 1, 1885, pp. 20, 23, 24, 32,.

11. Eckel, Edwin B., *Minerals of Colorado*, Friends of Mineralogy – Colorado, Fulcrum Publishing Company, pp. 241-242, 1997.

12. Burchard, H. C., *Report of the Director of the Mint upon the production of precious metals in the United States in 1882* as reported in Henderson, Charles W., *Mining in Colorado*, U. S. Geological Survey Professional Paper 138, 1926, p. 204.

13. Burchard, H. C., *Report of the Director of the Mint upon the production of precious metals in the United States in 1884* as reported in Henderson, Charles W., *Mining in Colorado*, U. S. Geological Survey Professional Paper 138, 1926, p. 204-205.

14. *The San Luis Valley Historian*, 1983, Volume XV, Number 3, Werner, M. Ed, *Summitville: An Extended Talk About the Camp from the Saguache Chronicle, July 13, 1883*, pp. 18-20.

15. Henderson, Charles, W., *Mining in Colorado*, U. S. Geological Survey Professional Paper 138, pp. 202-205, 1926.

16. Ellithorpe, Ralph C., "Poker, Politics and Gold," *Denver Westerners Brand Book* (1971), The Denver Westerners, Inc.

17. Rio Grande County Clerk and Recorders Records, Book 4, p. 367, May 29, 1876.

18. General Land Office Records

19. Rio Grande County Clerk and Recorders Records, Book 4, p. 877, August 1876

20. Letter to author from Louise Colville dated March 6, 2011 – P. J. Peterson diary.

21. Rio Grande County Clerk's Record Book 5, p. 243.

22. General Land Office Records

23. *Colorado Weekly Pueblo Chieftain*, August 2, 1877.

24. Rio Grande County Clerk's Record Book 1, p.685

25. *Colorado Weekly Pueblo Chieftain*, August 2, 1877.

26. Rio Grande County Clerk's Record Book 3, p. 549.

27. *American National Biography*, Auspices of the American Council of Learned Societies, New York, Oxford University Press, 1999.

28. Ellithorpe, Ralph C., "Poker, Politics and Gold," *Denver Westerners Brand Book* (1971), The Denver Westerners, Inc., pp. 63-64.

29. Ibid., p. 64.

30. *American National Biography*, Auspices of the American Council of Learned Societies, New York, Oxford University Press, 1999.

31. Riggenbach, Emma M., *A Bridge to Yesterday*, Monte Vista, Colorado, High Valley Press, 1982, p. 299.

32. Ellithorpe, Ralph C., "Poker, Politics and Gold," *Denver Westerners Brand Book* (1971), The Denver Westerners, Inc., p. 51.

33. Raymond, R. W., *Statistics of Mines and Mining in the States and Territories West of the Rocky Mountains for 1875* as reported in Henderson, Charles W., *Mining in Colorado*, U. S. Geological Survey Professional Paper 138, 1926, p. 203.

34. Newspaper article and information on literary society from Louise Colville on June 6 and July 5, 2011.

35. *The San Luis Valley Historian*, 1983, Volume XV, Number 3, Werner, M. Ed, *Summitville: An Extended Talk About the Camp from the Saguache Chronicle, July 13, 1883*, pp. 18-20.

36. *The Colorado Mining Directory*, 1883, p. 588.

37. Wolle, Muriel Sibell, *Stampede to Timberline*, Sponsored by The University of Colorado, 1949, p. 315.

38. *The San Luis Valley Historian*, 1998, Volume XXX, Number 3, "The Barlow and Sanderson Stage Line in the San Luis Valley," pp. 9-10.

39. *The San Luis Valley Historian*, 1975, Volume VII, Number 2, "Military Wagon Road from Alamosa to Pagosa Springs" *(Denver Daily Tribune,* December 10, 1878*)*, pp. 13-15.

40. *The San Luis Valley Historian*, 1975, Volume VII, Number 2, A Letter from Walter Comly to his Mother – 1882, p, 19.

41. *The San Luis Valley Historian*, 1975, Volume VII, Number 2, A Letter from Walter Comly to his Father – 1882, p. 21.

42. Williams, Hattie F., *The Gold Brick Holdup*, Colorful Colorado, Territorial Daughters of Colorado.

CHAPTER THREE – SLOW TIMES

1. Wolle, Muriel Sibell, *Stampede to Timberline*, Sponsored by the University of Colorado, 1949, p. 315.

2. Ellithorpe, Ralph C., "Poker, Politics and Gold," *Denver Westerners Brand Book* (1971), The Denver Westerners, Inc., p. 92.

3. Scamehorn, Lee, *Albert Eugene Reynolds - Colorado's Mining King*, 1995, p. 130.

4. Ellithorpe, Ralph C., "Poker, Politics and Gold," *Denver Westerners Brand Book* (1971), The Denver Westerners, Inc., p. 85.

5. Scamehorn, Lee, *Albert Eugene Reynolds - Colorado's Mining King*, 1995, p. 130.

6. Ellithorpe, Ralph C., "Poker, Politics and Gold," *Denver Westerners Brand Book* (1971), The Denver Westerners, Inc., p. 89.

7. Ibid., p. 89.

8. Scamehorn, Lee, *Albert Eugene Reynolds - Colorado's Mining King*, 1995, p. 17.

9. Ewing, Charles R. W. and Smith, Claude, *Report on the Little Annie Group of Mines, Summit Mining District, Rio Grande County, Colorado*, Colorado School of Mines Graduation Thesis, 1900, p. 1.

10. Ibid., p. 21.

11. Ibid., pp. 23-24.

12. Ibid., pp. 24-25.

13. *Mineral Resources of the United States*, 1922, pp. 544-545.

14. Scamehorn, Lee, *Albert Eugene Reynolds - Colorado's Mining King*, 1995, p. 174

15. Ibid., p. 198.

16. *Mineral Resources of the United States*, 1923, pp. 614 and 636.

17. *Mineral Resources of the United States*, 1924, p.550.

18. Scamehorn, Lee, *Albert Eugene Reynolds - Colorado's Mining King*, 1995, p. 222.

CHAPTER FOUR – REBIRTH

1. Colorado Mining Association, *Annual Yearbook for 1936*, "Summitville-Colorado's Sensational Gold Camp."

2. Walker, Wayne T., "Jack Pickens–Man With a Secret," *True West*, Jan/Feb 1977, pp. 28-29.

3. *The San Luis Valley Historian*, 1974, Volume VI, Number 4, Secret kept 24 years leads Del Norte prospector and miner to riches, pp. 38-44.

4. Scamehorn, Lee, *Albert Eugene Reynolds – Colorado's Mining King*, 1995, pp. 221-222.

5. *Ben Poxson, A Reminiscence*, unpublished transcript, 1988, p. 24.

6. *The San Luis Valley Historian*, Volume XXII, Number 1, "History of the Summitville Mining District by Deanna R. Shriver, 1965," 1990, pp. 4-38. (Note: words in quotations are Pickens words as quoted by Elmer Underwood of Del Norte in an interview with Shriver.)

7. *The San Luis Valley Historian*, Volume VI, Number 4, Secret kept 24 years leads Del Norte prospector and miner to riches, 1974, pp. 38-44.

8. *Ben Poxson, A Reminiscence*, unpublished transcript, 1988, p. 26.

9. Letter from V. W. "Bill" Ellithorpe to the author dated March 11, 2011.

10. Ellithorpe, Ralph C., "Poker, Politics and Gold," *Denver Westerners Brand Book* (1971), The Denver Westerners, Inc., pp. 97-99.

11. *Mineral Resources of the U.S.*, 1927, p. 558 and 1928, p. 845.

12. Scamehorn, Lee, *Albert Eugene Reynolds– Colorado's Mining King*, 1995, p.223.

13. Ibid., p. 223.

14. Ibid., p. 226.

15. Ibid., p. 227.

16. Summitville annual report for 1933 to the Colorado Bureau of Mines.

17. *The Rocky Mountain News*, August 1, 1990.

18. Scamehorn, Lee, *Albert Eugene Reynolds– Colorado's Mining King*, 1995, p.227.

19. Knight Piesold and Company, *Chronological Site History, Summitville Mine, Rio Grande County, Colorado*, Volume I, 1993, pp. 17-18.

20. *Mineral Resources of the U.S.*, 1934.

21. Colorado Mining Association *1936 Annual Yearbook*, p. 24.

22. Knight Piesold and Company, *Chronological Site History, Summitville Mine, Rio Grande County, Colorado*, Volume I, 1993, pp. 17-18.

23. Colorado Mining Association *1936 Annual Yearbook*, "Summitville – Colorado's Sensational Gold Camp."

24. Knight Piesold and Company, *Chronological Site History, Summitville Mine, Rio Grande County, Colorado*, Volume I, 1993, pp. 17-18.

25. Letter to W. C. Heath, Vice President, A. O. Smith Corporation from Ben T. Poxson, dated March 18, 1936.

26. Guiteras, Jos. R., *Mining and Milling Methods and Costs at the Summitville Cons. Mines, Inc., Summitville, Colorado*, U.S. Bureau of Mines I. C. 6990, August 1938, p. 22.

27. Letter from V. W. "Bill" Ellithorpe to the author dated May 4, 2001 and *Mineral Resources of the U. S.*, 1937, pp. 331-332.

28. Colorado Mining Association *1936 Annual Yearbook*, "Summitville – Colorado's Sensational Gold Camp."

29. Summitville 1937 Annual Report to the Colorado Bureau of Mines

30. Letter to George H. Garrey from Edward Thornton, General Superintendent, Summitville Consolidated Mines, Inc, dated May 25, 1935.

31. Knight Piesold and Company, *Chronological Site History, Summitville Mine, Rio Grande County, Colorado*, Volume I, 1993, pp. 17-18.

32. Guiteras, Jos. R., *Mining and Milling Methods and Costs at the Summitville Cons. Mines, Inc., Summitville, Colorado*, U.S. Bureau of Mines I. C. 6990, August 1938. p. 11.

33. *Mineral Resources of the U. S.*, 1938, p. 275.

34. *Mineral Resources of the U. S.*, 1939, p. 301.

35. Colorado Mining Association *1940 Annual Yearbook*, "Summitville."

36. Knight Piesold and Company, *Chronological Site History, Summitville Mine, Rio Grande County, Colorado*, Volume I, 1993, p. 19.

37. Letter to the secretary of Summitville Mines Corporation from the secretary of Summitville Consolidated Mines, Inc., dated February 6, 1942.

38. *Engineering and Mining Journal*, Volume 143, February 1942, p. 116.

39. *Mineral Resources of the U. S.*, 1942, p. 339.

40. Scamehorn, Lee, *Albert Eugene Reynolds–Colorado's Mining King*, 1995, p. 228.
41. *Mineral Resources of the U. S.*, 1944, p. 320.
42. Knight Piesold and Company, *Chronological Site History, Summitville Mine, Rio Grande County, Colorado*, Volume I, 1993, p. 19.
43. Colorado Mining Association *1946 Annual Yearbook*, "Summitville, Rio Grande County."
44. *Mineral Resources of the U. S.*, 1944, p. 1407.
45. *Mineral Resources of the U. S.*, 1948, p. 1465.
46. *Mineral Resources of the U. S.*, 1949, p. 1438.
47. Eberhart, Perry, *Guide to the Colorado Ghost Towns and Mining Camps*, Sage Books, 1959, p. 412.
48. Bancroft, Caroline, *Colorful Colorado: Its Dramatic History*, Sage Books, 1958, p. 82.
49. Arlie Stanger's memories given to the author February 2010.
50. Raylene Williams Owen's memories given to the author May 31, 2010.
51. Letter from V. W. "Bill" Ellithorpe to the author dated March 11, 2011.

CHAPTER FIVE – LIMITED PRODUCTION AND EXPLORATION

1. Colorado Bureau of Mines *1954 Annual Report*, p. 24.
2. *Mineral Resources of the U. S.*, 1954, p. 290.
3. *Mineral Resources of the U. S.*, 1955, p. 283.
4. Ellithorpe, Ralph C., "Poker, Politics and Gold," *Denver Westerners Brand Book* (1971), The Denver Westerners, Inc., p. 109.
5. Colorado Mining Association *1958 Annual Yearbook*, "Rio Grande County."
6. Colorado Mining Association *1960 Annual Yearbook*, "Rio Grande County."
7. *The San Luis Valley Historian*, Volume XXII, Number 1, "History of the Summitville Mining District by Deanna Shriver, 1965," 1990, pp. 4-38.

8. Unknown Author, *Brief History of the Emperius Mining Company*, March 10, 1972.

9. Scamehorn, Lee, *Albert Eugene Reynolds–Colorado's Mining King*, 1995, p. 228

10. Interview with Charles E. Melbye on May 27, 2010.

11. Colorado Bureau of Mines *1963 Annual Report*, p. 36.

12. Colorado Bureau of Mines *1964 Annual Report*, p. 37.

13. Colorado Bureau of Mines *1966 Annual Report*, p. 51.

14. Interview with Charles E. Melbye on May 27, 2010.

15. Colorado Bureau of Mines *1967 Annual Report*, p. 36.

16. *The San Luis Valley Historian*, 1990, Volume XXII, Number 1, "Summitville Mining and Exploration, 1965-1989" by Mark F. Coolbaugh.

17. *Mineral Resources of the U. S.*, 1968, p. 164.

18. *Mineral Resources of the U. S.*, 1969, p. 172.

19. Letter from Tom Bond III to the author dated March 4, 2010.

20. Eckel, Edwin B., *Minerals of Colorado*, 1997, p. 171.

21. *The San Luis Valley Historian*, 1990, Volume XXII, Number 1, "Summitville Mining and Exploration, 1965-1989" by Mark F. Coolbaugh.

22. Colorado Bureau of Mines *1970 Annual Report*, p. 21 and 42.

23. Colorado Bureau of Mines *1971 Annual Report*, p. 19 and 41.

24. *Mineral Resources of the U. S.*, 1972, p. 151.

25. Letter from Tom Bond III to the author dated March 4, 2010.

26. Letter from Charles E. Melbye to the author dated June 4, 2010.

27. *The San Luis Valley Historian*, 1990, Volume XXII, Number 1, *Summitville Mining and Exploration, 1965-1989 by Mark F. Coolbaugh.*

28. Scamehorn, Lee, *Albert Eugene Reynolds–Colorado's Mining King*, 1995, p. 229.

29. *The San Luis Valley Historian*, 1990, Volume XXII, Number1, *Summitville Mining and Exploration, 1965-1989 by Mark F. Coolbaugh.*

30. *The San Luis Valley Historian*, 1990, Volume XXII, Number 1, *The Gold Boulder*, pp. 4-38.

31. *The San Luis Valley Historian*, 1990, Volume XXII, Number 1, *Summitville Mining and Exploration, 1965-1989 by Mark F. Coolbaugh*.

32. Letter from V. W. "Bill" Ellithorpe to the author on March 11, 2011.

33. *The Pueblo Chieftain*, "Anaconda Geologist Speaks Out on Summitville Operations, June 24, 1981."

34. *Mineral Resources of the U. S.* 1984, p. 124.

CHAPTER SIX – GALACTIC RESOURCES, INC.

1. *Mineral Resources of the U. S.*, 1984, p. 124.

2. *The San Luis Valley Historian*, Volume XXII, Number 1, "1984-1989 Open-Pit – Heap Leach Gold Mining" by Galactic Resources, Inc., 1990, pp. 4-38.

3. Scamehorn, Lee, *Albert Eugene Reynolds–Colorado's Mining King*, 1995, p. 231.

4. Knight Piesold and Company, *Chronological Site History – Summitville Mine, Rio Grande County, Colorado*, Volume I prepared for the Summitville Study Group, 1993, p. 24.

5. *The San Luis Valley Historian*, Volume XXII, Number 1, "1984-1989 Open-Pit – Heap Leach Gold Mining" by Galactic Resources, Inc., 1990, pp. 4-38.

6. Knight Piesold and Company, *Chronological Site History – Summitville Mine, Rio Grande County, Colorado*, Volume I prepared for the Summitville Study Group, 1993, p. 25.

7. Danielson, Luke and McNamara, Alix, "The Summitville: What Went Wrong," *Colorado Department of Natural Resources*, March 25, 1993, pp. 2-3.

8. Vanderwilt, John W., Colorado Mineral Resources Board, *Mineral Resources of Colorado*, 1947, p. 185.

9. McNulty, Dr. Terence P., *The Relative Scale and Impacts of Mining Activities and Operations from 1870 through 1992 at the Summitville Mine Site*, 2001(data from Galactic operations only.)

10. Peele, Robert, *Mining Engineer's Handbook*, Volume II, "Section 33 – Gold Amalgamation and Cyanidation," 1950, p. 33-06.

11. Knight Piesold and Company, *Chronological Site History – Summitville Mine, Rio Grande County, Colorado*, Volume I prepared for the Summitville Study Group, 1993, p. 34.

12. *The San Luis Valley Historian*, 1990, Volume XXII, Number 1, "Summitville Mining and Exploration, 1965-1989" by Mark F. Coolbaugh.

13. Knight Piesold and Company, *Chronological Site History – Summitville Mine, Rio Grande County, Colorado*, Volume I prepared for the Summitville Study Group, 1993, Executive Summary.

14. *The Engineering and Mining Journal*, March 1993, p. 16BB.

BIBLIOGRAPHY

GOVERNMENT DOCUMENTS
Federal

Henderson, Charles W., *Mining in Colorado*, U.S. Geological Survey Professional paper 138, 1926.

Steven, Thomas A., and Ratte', James C., *Geology and Ore Deposits of the Summitville District, San Juan Mountains, Colorado*, U. S. Geological survey Professional Paper 343, 1960.

Steven, Thomas A. and Lipman, Peter W., *Calderas of the San Juan Volcanic Field*, U. S. Geological Survey Professional paper 958, 1976.

King, Trude V. V., Editor, *Environmental Considerations of Active and Abandoned Mine Lands: Lessons from Summitville, Colorado*, U. S. Geological survey Bulletin 2220, pp. 8-9, 1995.

Guiteras, Jos. R., *Mining and Milling Methods and Costs at the Summitville Cons. Mines, Inc., Summitville, C*olorado, U. S. Bureau of Mines Informational Circular 6990, August 1938.

General Land Office Records, U. S. Bureau of Land Management.

Mineral Resources of the United States, U. S. Geological Survey.

State of Colorado

Vanderwilt, John W., Colorado Mineral Resources Board, *Mineral Resources of Colorado*, 1947.

Neubert, John, *Geology of the Upper Alamosa River Area*, Colorado Geological Survey Rock Talk, Volume 4, Number 2, April 2001, 2001.

Pendleton, James A., Posey, Harry H. and Long, Michael B., *Characterizing Summitville and Its Impacts: Setting the Scene*, Colorado Geological Survey Special Publication 38, 1995.

The Colorado Mining Directory (1883).

Summitville Annual Report to the Colorado Bureau of Mines.

Colorado Bureau of Mines Annual Reports.

Rio Grande County, Colorado

Rio Grande County Clerk and Recorder's Records

PROFESSIONAL JOURNALS

Hills, R. C., *Ore Deposits of Summit District, Rio Grande County, Colorado*, Scientific Society Proceedings, Volume 1, 1885.

Stoffgren, Roger, *Genesis of Acid-Sulfate Alteration and Gold-Copper-Silver Mineralization at Summitville, Colorado*, Economic Geology, Volume 82, 1985.

Gray, J. E. and Coolbaugh, Mark F., *Geology and Geochemistry of Summitville, Colorado: An Epithermal Acid Sulfate Deposit in a Volcanic Dome*, Economic Geology, Volume 89, 1994.

MINING JOURNALS

Colorado Mining Association Yearbooks
The Engineering and Mining Journal

MAGAZINES

The San Luis Valley Historian, 1969, Volume I, Number 2, Dates, p. 15.

The San Luis Valley Historian, 1974, Volume VI, Number 4, Secret kept 24 years leads Del Norte prospector and miner to riches.

The San Luis Valley Historian, 1975, Volume VII, Number 2, *Military Wagon Road from Alamosa to Pagosa Springs* (*Denver Daily Tribune*, December 10, 1878).

The San Luis Valley Historian, 1975, Volume VII, Number 2, A Letter from Walter Comly to his Mother – 1882.

The San Luis Valley Historian, 1975, Volume VII, Number 2, A Letter from Walter Comly to his Father – 1882.

The San Luis Valley Historian, 1976, Volume VIII, Number 2, *San Juan Prospector* clippings from Rebecca Shaw scrapbook of the 1880s and 90s.

The San Luis Valley Historian, 1976, Volume VIII, Number 1, "The Diary of J. Cary French, 1871, Part1."

The San Luis Valley Historian, 1976, Volume VIII, Number 2, "The Diary of J. Carey French, 1871, Part 2."

The San Luis Valley Historian, 1978, Volume X, Number 3, Snowfall of 1883-1884.

The San Luis Valley Historian, 1982, Volume XIV, Number 4, "The Hayden Survey in the San Luis Valley, 1873-1876."

The San Luis Valley Historian, 1965, Volume XXII, Number 1, "History of the Summitville Mining District" by Deanna R. Shriver.

The San Luis Valley Historian, 1990, Volume XXII, Number 1, "Summitville Mining and Exploration, 1965-1989" by Mark F. Coolbaugh.

The San Luis Valley Historian, 1990, Volume XXII, Number 1, "1984-1989 Open-Pit Heap Leach Gold Mining" by Galactic Resources, Inc.

The San Luis Valley Historian, 1990, Volume XXII, Number 1, "The Gold Boulder."

The San Luis Valley Historian, 1995, Volume XXVII, Number 4.

The San Luis Valley Historian, 1998, Volume XXX, Number 2, "Whence the Windsor Hotel."

The San Luis Valley Historian, 1998, Volume XXX, Number 3, "The Barlow and Sanderson Stage Line in the San Luis Valley."

Colorado Magazine, "Pioneering in the San Juan," Welch Nossaman, October 1957.

True West, Jack Pickens – "Man With a Secret," Walker, Wayne T., Jan/Feb 1977.

NEWSPAPERS

The Denver Post
The Rocky Mountain News
The Pueblo Chieftain
Western Gazette
Colorado Weekly Pueblo Chieftain
The Del Norte Prospector
The San Juan Prospector

BOOKS

American National Biography, Auspices of the American Council of Learned Societies, New York, Oxford University Press, 1999.

Athearn, Robert G., *Rebel of the Rockies: A History of the Denver and Rio Grande Western Railroad*, Yale University Press, 1962.

Bancroft, Caroline, *Colorful Colorado: Its Dramatic History*, Sage Books, 1958.

Eberhart, Perry, *Guide to the Colorado Ghost Towns and Mining Camps*, Sage Books, 1959.

Eckel, Edwin B., *Minerals of Colorado*, Friends of Mineralogy – Colorado, Fulcrum Publishing, 1997.

Elllithorpe, Ralph C., "Poker, Politics and Gold," *Denver Westerners Brand Book* (1971), The Denver Westerners, Inc.

Hafen, LeRoy PhD, *Colorado and Its People*, Volume II, Lewis Historical Publishing Company.

Huston, Richard C., *A Silver Camp Called Creede*, Western Reflections Publishing Company, 2005.

Peele, Robert, *Mining Engineer's Handbook*, Volume II, Section 33 – Gold Amalgamation and Cyanidation, 1950.

Riggenbach, Emma M., *A Bridge to Yesterday*, High Valley Press, 1982.

Scamehorn, Lee, *Albert Eugene Reynolds - Colorado's Mining King*, University of Oklahoma Press, 1995.

Spencer, Frank C., *The Story of the San Luis Valley*, San Luis Valley Historical Society, 1975.

Taggert, Arthur F., *Elements of Ore Dressing*, John Wiley & Sons, Inc., 1951.

Williams, Hattie F., *The Gold Brick Holdup*, Colorful Colorado, Territorial Daughters of Colorado.

Wolle, Muriel Sibell, *Stampede to Timberline*, Sponsored by the University of Colorado, 1949.

McCarty, Florence, *To Catch A Star*, High Valley Press, 1996.

UNPUBLISHED MATERIAL

Espinosa, Fred, *Del Norte – Its Past and Present*, mimeograph paper, Del Norte Chamber of Commerce, 1963.

Ewing, Charles R W. and Smith, Claude, *Report on the Little Annie Group of Mines, Summit Mining District, Rio Grande County, Colorado*, Colorado School of Mines Graduation Thesis, 1900.

Knight Piesold and Company, *Chronological Site History, Summitville Mine, Rio Grande County, Colorado*, Volume I, 1993.

McNulty, Dr. Terence P., *The Relative Scale and Impacts of Mining Activities and Operations from 1870 through 1992 at the Summitville Mine Site*, 2001.

Ben Poxson, *A Reminiscence*, unpublished transcript, 1988.

Unknown Author, *Brief History of the Emperius Mining Company*, March 10, 1972.

Letter to W. C. Heath, Vice President, A. O. Smith Corporation from Ben T. Poxson, dated March 18. 1936.

Letter to George H. Garrey from Edward Thornton, General Superintendent, Summitville Consolidated Mines, Inc., dated May 25, 1935.

Letter to the secretary of Summitville Mines Corporation from the secretary of Summitville Consolidated Mines, Inc., dated February 6, 1942.

CORRESPONDENCE AND INTERVIEWS

Bond II, Tom, correspondence, 2010.

Colville, Louise, correspondence and interview, 2011.

Ellithorpe, V. W. "Bill", correspondence, pictures and interviews, 2011

Melbye, Charles, correspondence and interviews, 2010.

Owens, Raylene Williams, correspondence and memories, 2010.

Stanger, Arlie, correspondence, pictures and memories, 2010.

Index

A. O. Smith Corporation, 92
Adams, Alva, 57
Adams, Charles, 29
Adams, Dr. R. F., 28, 45
Adams. Maynard Cornett, 2
Agency for Toxic Substances & Disease Registry, 142
AMAX, Inc., 139
American Concentrator Company, 79
American Smelting and Refining Company (ASARCO), 132-133
Anaconda Minerals Company, 133, 134, 139
Arthur G. McKee Construction Company, 129
Aztec Company, 52
Barlow and Sanderson, 65
Barnsdall Corporation, 80
Barnsdall, Theodore N., 72, 73, 75-76, 78
Beamer, J. L., 57
Bechtel Civil and Minerals, Inc., 140
Bethke, Phillip, 12
Beverly, C. E., 133, 135-136
Bill Bird and Associates, 132, 133
Black, Barney, 115, 116
Bockhaus, Louie, 2
Bond, Tom III, 23, 129-130
Bowen Bonanza Mining Company, 58
Bowen, Thomas M., 2, 45, 47, 54, 55, 56, 58-60, 76
Brandt, Ferdinand H., 26, 27, 28, 43, 54
Brunot Treaty, 2
Bull Dog Mining Company, 53
Buqui, 133
Burchard, H. C., 47-48, 50
Burris, Columbus W., 56
Burton, Arthur, 57
Carruthers, Mary Jane, 114
Civilian Conservation Corps, 95
Clark, Frank, 77
Clark, Lewis, 54
Cleghorn, John, 36
Cleveland-Cliffs Iron Company, 129, 131
Colorado Hayden Survey, 11
Colorado Mined Land Reclamation Division of the Department of Natural Resources, 140, 149
Colville, Louise, 7
Comley, Walter, 66-67
Conejos County, 27, 28
Consolidated Gold Mining Corporation, 78
Coolbaugh, Mark, 12
Cooper, Marville W., 55, 78
Crawford, George, 78
Cripple Creek & Victor Gold Mining Company, 142
Crook, John J., 54, 57
Cumbres Pass, 18, 20
Darley, Reverend Alexander, 46
Davies, Kathryn Airy, 116
Dayton, Stanley H., 143-146

Del Norte, 2, 36, 65
Denver Museum of Natural History, 137
Detrick, H. F., 98, 104, 105
Dodge, LeGrande, 54
Eberhart, Perry, 2
Eckel, Edwin, 49
Edstrom, Andrew, 7
Ellithorpe, Harry V., 7, 22, 123
Ellithorpe, Ralph C. 7, 22, 97, 123
Ellithorpe, Robert M. "Bob", 134, 135, 136
Ellithorpe, V. W. "Bill", 7, 87-88, 117, 123, 134, 136
Endlich, F. M., 11
Environmental Protection Agency, 146, 152, 153
Erickson, Homer, 4
Esmond, John, 27-28
Esmond Mine, 42
Fertig, Wendell W., 6
Frenchmen, 1-2
French, J. Cary, 26-27, 30-36
Friedland, Robert, 139
Frontier Resources, 131
Galactic Resources, Inc., 139
Galactic Resources Limited, 139, 152
Gates, Martin, 113, 114, 115
Gates, Melvin, 114, 115
Garrey, George H., 80, 90, 91, 92-93, 101, 127
General Minerals Corporation, 127, 128
Golconda Gold Mining Company, 48, 56-57, 76
Gold Links Mining Company, 6, 101, 103, 127
Gold Reserve Act of 1934, 82, 138
Golden Cycle Corporation, 89-90
Golden Star Gold & Silver Mining Company, 57
Goupil, Theodore, 28, 42
Grant, John, 29
Gray, John E. 12
Green, Grover, 124
Guiteras, Jos. R., 98
Hanks, Mrs., 6
Hartford Gold Extraction Company, 79
Henderson, Charles W., 7
Hills, R. C., 11, 48-49
Hold, Henry S., 55
Howard, Alan, 6
Hoyt, Henry S. Jr., 54, 78
Hutchinson, Irene Duncan, 115
Iowa & Colorado Consolidated Company, 44, 49-50, 55-56
Jasper Mining District, 15
Jones and Nylene, 103
Keyes, Thomas, 28
King, John R., 133
King, Trude V.V., 12
Kirby, Dan, 79
Kuhn, Frances, 123
La Loma, 26-27
Lewis, Gunny, 22
Lipman, Peter W., 12
Little Annie Mines, 39, 54, 79
Little Annie Gold Mining Company, 50, 54, 67, 70

Little Jessie Segregated Mining Company, 58
Livermore, John, 127
Livingston, Johnston, 54, 55, 57
Macatee, Gordon, 117
Mann, Josiah, 29
Martin, A. E., 56
McAtee, W. I., 127
McCarty, Florence, 117-119
McFadzean, Dr. 77
McNeil, John L., 78
McWilliams, 123-124
Melbye, Charles E., 128, 129
Monte Vista, 1, 2
Montoya, Luis, 45
Morey and Sperry, 53
Morse, Anna Reynolds, 91
Morse, Bradish, 90-91
Myers, Robert, 113, 114
Naslund, Mary, 46
Newlon, Paul, 104, 105
Newmont Mining Company, 16, 127
Nossaman, Welch, 20-22
Odin Gold Mining Company, 57
OK Company, 26
Owen, Raylene McWilliams, 7, 123-125
Palmer, Charles P., 76
Palmer, Henry E., 55
Parker, Harriet, 114, 115
Patton, Horace B., 11
Peterson, P. J., 7, 26, 27, 28, 29-30, 53, 54, 64
Persson, Louis, 46
Pfeiffer, Colonel Albert, 3
Pickens, John W. "Jack", 80, 83-90

Polaris Resources, 131
Posey, O. P., 29, 57
Poxson, Benjamin T., 86, 87, 92-93, 97, 101, 127, 128
Project Works Administration, 95
Quad Construction, 131
Ratte', James C., 7, 11
Raymond, R. W., 25-26, 37-39, 61
Reef, J. S., 57
Reynolds, Albert Eugene, 72, 73-75, 76, 78, 79, 80, 98, 142
Reynolds Mining Company, 132, 133, 139
Reynolds-Morse Corporation, 80, 90, 127, 128, 132
Rigg, John B. "Jack", 127, 128
Rio Grande County, 2, 25, 73, 95, 106
Rio Grande Railroad, 46
Roach, Alf R., 78
Robins, C. E., 39-42, 54
Rye, Robert O., 12
San Juan Consolidated Mining Company, 45, 52-54, 58
Scarff, John, 77
Shaw, Frank L., 89
Sherman Silver Purchase Act of 1890, 72 and repeal in 1893, 72-73, 74
Siegfried, Frank E., 127
Silver Act of 1934, 82-83
Sloan, Thomas, 55, 78
Smith, F. R., 92
Smith, Prof. J. Alden, 53-54
South Mountain, 27, 42

South Mountain Mining Company, 127
Stanger, Arlie, 7, 22-23, 120-123
Stanger, Frank, 120
Stanger, Herb, 119-120
Stanger, Kenneth, 8, 119
Steven, Thomas A., 7, 12
Stoffgren, Roger, 12
Stunner Pass Overview, 16-17
Summit District, 11, 25, 27, 28
Summitville Living Conditions, 113-125
Summitville Townsite, 61-62, 64-65, 72, 107-113, 128
Summitville Consolidated Mines, Inc., 92-93, 95, 97, 98, 101, 104, 149
Summitville Consolidated Mining Company, 140, 141, 151
Summitville Gold Mines, Inc., 91
Summitville Mines Corporation, 91
Summitville Mining Company, 103
Summitville Mining District, 2, 11, 16, 27
Taylor, Charles W., 56
Thornton, Edward, 95, 106
Treasure Mountain, 1
Tyrrel, Homer, 4
Union Pacific Mining Company, 129
Valdez, Juanita, 27
Van Gieson, William, 57
Vikre, Peter G., 12
Water Quality Control Division of the Colorado Department of Health, 152
War Production Board Order 208, 102, 103
Warriner, L., 95
Werner, M. Ed, 50-51, 64-65
Western Industrial and Investigating Service, 104
Wightman Fork, 5, 10, 27, 46, 97
Wiley, Judge Jessie C., 80, 84-86, 89-90
Winchester, E. S., 54
Winchester, Lucius, 54
Winchester, L. W., 58
Withrow and Warr Lease, 80
Wolf Creek Pass, 2, 18-19
W. S. Moore Company, 129, 131
Ydren, Charles. 46
Zeiler, Harry, 113, 114, 115

CPSIA information can be obtained at www.ICGtesting.com
Printed in the USA
LVOW11s0211120414

381438LV00002B/18/P